409581LV00008B/8
CMF:COLORSTD
PERFECT

409581LVX00005BA - 409581LVX00005BA [1 : 1]

* 4 0 9 5 8 1 L V 0 0 0 0 8 B *

BOOK
STCO19_SM
REWORK
Beard,Sadie_ :

Oce Operator's Name (Please print)

_____

* 4 0 9 5 8 1 L V *

Printed at: Mon Oct 20 17:25:28 2014 on device lvoce02-86

Batch 409581LV00008B

| 409581LVX00005BA | 9781910547007 | Alaskan Klee Kai Ultimate Care Guide I |
| PERFECT | 6.00X9.00 | 198   (1) |

Academic Search Engines

CHANDOS
INFORMATION PROFESSIONAL SERIES

Series Editor: Ruth Rikowski
(email: Rikowskigr@aol.com)

Chandos' new series of books is aimed at the busy information professional. They have been specially commissioned to provide the reader with an authoritative view of current thinking. They are designed to provide easy-to-read and (most importantly) practical coverage of topics that are of interest to librarians and other information professionals. If you would like a full listing of current and forthcoming titles, please visit www.chandospublishing.com.

New authors: we are always pleased to receive ideas for new titles; if you would like to write a book for Chandos, please contact Dr Glyn Jones on g.jones.2@elsevier.com or telephone +44 (0) 1865 843000.

Academic Search Engines

A quantitative outlook

José Luis Ortega

ELSEVIER

AMSTERDAM • BOSTON • CAMBRIDGE • HEIDELBERG • LONDON
NEW YORK • OXFORD • PARIS • SAN DIEGO
SAN FRANCISCO • SINGAPORE • SYDNEY • TOKYO
Chandos Publishing is an imprint of Elsevier

CHANDOS
PUBLISHING

Chandos Publishing
Elsevier Limited
The Boulevard
Langford Lane
Kidlington
Oxford OX5 1GB
UK
store.elsevier.com/Chandos-Publishing-/IMP_207/

Chandos Publishing is an imprint of Elsevier Limited

Tel: +44 (0) 1865 843000
Fax: +44 (0) 1865 843010
store.elsevier.com

First published in 2014

ISBN 978-1-84334-791-0 (print)
ISBN 978-1-78063-472-2 (online)

Chandos Information Professional Series ISSN: 2052-210X (print) and ISSN: 2052-2118 (online)

Library of Congress Control Number: 2014946174

© J.L. Ortega, 2014

Typeset by Domex e-Data Pvt. Ltd., India
Printed in the UK and USA.

Transferred to Digital Printing in 2014

To everyone who was interested in this book – family,
friends, colleagues – and especially
mi madre y mi padre, quienes se empeñaron en que este
libro saliera a la luz

Contents

List of figures and tables

Figures

Tables

Preface

In 1989 the World Wide Web was born in the CERN laboratory, a large and international scientific facility. It was not by chance that this information publishing technology appeared out of a scientific environment because researchers always have needed access to high-quality information about new advances as well as information on the state of the art of their disciplines. At the same time, the scientific community demands the sharing of media that help the rapid dissemination of results and discussion. Today, the practice of science would be impossible without a strong information system that allows the diffusion and storage of all the necessary knowledge. In this context, the Internet and the web represent an authentic revolution, comparable to the birth of the printing press, in the way in which scientists communicate among themselves. This new web era is also bringing about an explosion of new academic results that recognize the diversity of scholarly activity. But perhaps the most important change is the questioning of the earlier way of thinking typified by print publishing. The new potential of the web, participative and open, is favouring the break-up of publishing barriers when it comes to disseminating results. Thus, the open access movement, with the proliferation of digital libraries and repositories as well as the consolidation of free electronic journals, fights for a total democratization of science, bypassing intermediaries and reducing the cost of scientific publishing.

On the other hand, Web 2.0 has made possible a Science 2.0 where social networking sites have emerged that enhance the discussion and sharing of ideas, the comparison of curricula and the popularization of results. In this way, scientists are discovering a huge spectrum of utilities that expand the diffusion of results as well as improve their relationships with other partners. Alongside this flowering of new publishing forms, the web is also bringing about an important change in the evaluation of research. Webometrics – studying the use of hyperlinks as a reflection of citations, and of academic web pages as synonymous with research production – and currently Altmetrics – analysing the parallelism between citation impact and social visibility – are symptoms of the need for a new way to evaluate this changeable behaviour in research performance, breaking the borders of bibliometric impact and classical publication in print journals.

In this new scenario, specialized search engines for scientists have been emerging over the past few years as a means of gathering this new academic production, accessible via the web. Although academic search engines are indebted to classical citation indexes, this new publishing and communication panorama is changing the appearance of these search services, incorporating heterogeneous research results, adding information sharing tools, and offering a new perception on current scientific activity. In this way, these engines are springing up as web alternatives to the classical citation databases, mainly due to their free access, comprehensiveness and profiling applications.

In the face of such groundbreaking developments, this book aims to present a general review of the most important academic search engines in the market with the intention of making available a brief guide to how these platforms operate, to what and how many materials they index, and to which functionalities they support for a satisfactory search experience. This review has been carried out along a critical path discussing the suitability of these engines for the scientific community, their reliability for evaluation purposes, and the advantages and limitations of each service in meeting the specific and rigorous needs of the researchers. Further, this examination has been carried out via a precise analysis of every section and function, in which each searching feature has been explored and the sources that feed each tool have been tracked.

As the book's subtitle suggests, a quantitative approach is followed in this analytical review, with the aims of measuring the coverage and quantifying the weight of each source. However, the data obtained leads me to suggest an innovative methodology based on the profuse use of crawlers and harvesting procedures which draw a detailed picture of each search service. To some extent, it is an attempt to design an inverse engineering method to capture the essence of the data stored in those services – motivated by the fact that many search engines do not incorporate suitable search interfaces that allow users to take a global view on the coverage of the service as well as providing enough information about their functioning. Therefore, in many cases automatic queries were launched to secure the most detailed coverage possible of the search engine. Another important function of the crawling process is that it makes possible the detection of duplicated records and misleading information, and the absence of data on authors and documents. Thus, this work tries to present an objective analysis of these search tools, principally based on the extracted data.

Throughout the process of analysis of these products, it could be seen that many of them fulfil various concepts of what academic search engines are. My aim is to highlight the numerous forms that these services may take, signalling that there is no clear definition of what elements are essential in actually designating an academic search engine. The compilation of this list is driven by the popularity and the importance of these developments in shaping the concept of the academic search engine, although each element can differ markedly to the next. In this way, the intention is to present a colourful range of academic search solutions that illustrate different approaches to building data sets, designing search interfaces or structuring contents. On the other hand, the selection of these services has also been shaped by the fact that they share basic elements that reflect the principal characteristics of an academic search engine, helping to flesh out the meaning of the concept.

Addressing a topic in book form presents numerous problems, but publishing a work via web services is inevitably accompanied by the obsolescence of the results. Data on the size of search engines in terms of number of documents indexed, or on the disappearance/appearance of new functionalities, can change dramatically in a short period of time, even if a more quantitative approach is taken, where the data sets are the most unstable elements. For example, although all the figures in this book were updated during February and March 2014, it is possible that during the publication process many aspects will disappear or change. Thinking positively, this should be interpreted as a sign of the dynamic and evolving nature of scholarly engines.

For the above reason, I do not expect to have built a static picture of each search engine, but I hope that this quantitative approximation makes it possible to describe the fundamental characteristics and functionalities of each service, as well as to suggest their advantages and disadvantages for scientific users. An example of the problem of obsolescence mentioned above can be seen in the case of Scirus, which was closed down during the preparation of this book. Despite this, the analysis carried out on that product has been included in the book – first, as a final tribute to its contribution; second, because this could be the last analysis carried out on the site; and, third, because it is a good opportunity to explain for future reference how that engine worked.

About the author

José Luis Ortega is a web researcher in the Spanish National Research Council (CSIC). He achieved a fellowship in the Cybermetrics Lab of CSIC, where he finished his doctoral studies (2003–8). In 2005, he was employed by the Virtual Knowledge Studio of the Royal Netherlands Academy of Sciences and Arts, and in 2008 he took up a position as information scientist within CSIC. He now continues his collaboration with the Cybermetrics Lab in research areas such as webometrics, web usage mining, visualization of information, social network analysis and web bibliometrics.

Introduction

Abstract: This chapter first introduces the problem of the need for a clear definition of what an academic search engine is, and the colourful range of products that could be considered within this. The chapter goes on to summarize the mean characteristics that these engines should have in order to serve the complexity of scholarly information and the thoroughness of the scientific community. A brief history of these engines is given, marking their principal milestones and contributions, such as the appearance of the first autonomous citation index or the first author profiling platform. Finally, the chapter looks at the challenges these services will face in the future as they try to establish themselves within the landscape of research evaluation and information retrieval.

Key words: academic search engines, scientific users, autonomous citation indexing, profiling, research evaluation.

Academic search engines could be considered to be the meeting point between two streams that started to diverge just when the web evolved: on the one hand the traditional specialized databases and on the other hand the new generalist web search engines. Before the appearance of the web, any search product was a specialized object addressed to a specific and sophisticated user (scientist, technician, lawyer, etc.) who needed to carry out complex queries to obtain the highest precision or recall. These databases contained records with a great number of fields which described structured and formal documents. This paradigm started to break up when the arrival of the web brought about the opening up of these search services to a broad and heterogeneous population with few skills in information searching and with diverse needs. Thus, while the specialized databases retained their traditional search scheme, the new web search services began to adopt a search interface more suitable to their new users and the new hypertextual and multimedia documents, consistently simplifying the search pages (Lewandowski and Mayr, 2006). A good example of this transition was AltaVista, the first search engine on the web. The initial appearance of this service showed an advanced search with multiple boxes, Boolean operators and ranking criteria to display results, an unusual picture in the current scenario of increasingly accessible and user-friendly search interfaces (Figure 1.1). The arrival of Google in 1998 with its clear and simple search box, rapid response time and powerful crawling was the inflection point that definitively separated the world of search engines from the world of databases.

Nevertheless, the appearance of the academic search engines united these distant worlds again, creating a developed product focused on a concrete and specialized public, but based on the accessible information on the web. This new environment brought with it important challenges and a new conceptual framework, because these services should not be merely search engines of scientific information nor simply specialized databases running on the web, instead they should provide a new insight into scholarly information searchable on the web. In short, an academic search engine is neither a search engine nor a database – rather, it is the union of the best of both and, unfortunately, the mix of the complexities of each as well.

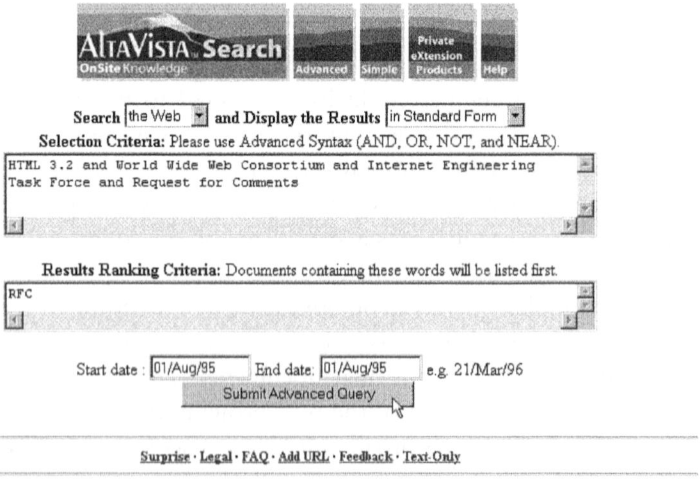

Figure 1.1   Advanced search in AltaVista (1996)

Source: (Ladd, 2000)

What is an academic search engine?

Firstly, it is necessary to provide a definition of an academic search engine, although this is not an easy task because the scientific literature in this area is rather sparse. Perhaps the simplest approach is to consider academic search engines as the search products that localize scientific information on the web (Codina, 2007). This is because, as will be seen, there are engines that act only as specialized search engines, indexing their data directly from the web and returning a clickable list, such as CiteSeer[x] and Google Scholar, and there are services that go beyond this to add elaborate and structured information – real assessment and benchmarking tools such as Microsoft Academic Search and AMiner, which incorporate functionalities to rank and measure the scientific activity; and there are services that are entirely lean on pre-processed data from secondary sources such as BASE or Q-Sensei Scholar, or systems that are supported entirely within their own means such as CiteSeer[x] and Google Scholar. This range of types and approaches comes from the reduced number of initiatives now on the web, and because each one starts from a particular view of the academic web search. Thus, although it is difficult to establish an outline definition, some measures can be made to distinguish a simple bibliographic database on the web from a real academic search engine. Therefore, such search services should be free web-based search services that incorporate added-value elements (citations, indicators, and so on) which allow their use for research evaluation, and should be open to different typologies of research results such as pre-prints, patents, presentations or teaching materials available on the web. Not all the products analysed in this book fit with this definition, but it is desirable that these elements are present in new and future developments.

Challenges for an academic search engine

Web-based products

As outlined above, the definition of an academic search engine is marked by its web context, which makes it different to traditional bibliographic databases. This singularity introduces some particularities inherent to the web environment. For instance, these engines are freely accessible on the web and therefore their contents can reach a broader audience, which increases the popularization of science and the appreciation for the scientific activity. However, this also provokes a higher public exposition and can prompt criticism of their functioning, coverage, searching and so on, as well as enabling the emergence of competitor developments.

A further aspect arising from the web context is that the volume of information has grown exponentially – hundreds of millions of web pages and documents related to scientific issues are now accessible. The enormous capability of these academic search engines reduces any manual data processing, so new automatic treatments are necessary in order to classify and index the amount of information generated. From a technical point of view, this is the sticking point of these search engines, because the quality of the services relies on the skill of developing autonomous processes that properly structure the data generated with as few mistakes as possible. The birth of autonomous citation indexes, the development of advanced parsing tools and the design of robust bots and harvesters are technical progressions which help the implementation of these engines but which, without a doubt, introduce failures in the citations counts, the identification of document elements and the disambiguation of names and titles.

These technical challenges are bigger still when the web information is not technically structured and presents multiple formal and informal scientific typologies. Unlike scientific databases, where the characteristics of each document are well-defined (author, title, venue, etc.) and the type of document is homogeneous (articles, notes, letters, etc.), the web gathers a great variety of documents (articles, presentations, theses, etc.) in unstructured formats where it is very difficult to distinguish between author, title, abstract, etc. This then requires a great technical effort to develop advanced parsing techniques that allow us to obtain the precise information on each document, as well as a wide and flexible data framework that enables the inclusion and characterization of any scientific document.

The need to overcome such problems is a necessary challenge for these initiatives because the quality of their product depends hugely on the technical solutions of these issues. In this sense, the way in which these matters are addressed makes these search services clear competitors of the traditional scientific databases due to their greater coverage and their ease of access.

Scientific users

An academic search engine is a specialized product which not only covers scientific information but is focused on a concrete user type: scientists. These users require search services which offer a range of instruments that not only allow them to locate precise and relevant information but that can also evaluate the quality of the information.

Unlike other users, scholars are simultaneously consumers and creators of content, which makes them more critical regarding coverage, the way in which the documents are indexed and the paper-author assignation – precisely because they can see how many of their own papers are indexed, whether they are correctly assigned to them, and whether their names are properly disambiguated. These personal insights can be one of the most important criteria for the refusal or acceptance of the use of a particular engine by a particular researcher.

The format and definition of the document type is very important, because the validity of its content is determined by the way in which the document was originated. Unlike general-interest search engines, where the content is more important than the container, in academic search engines the document typology is a quality indicator of the information that it contains. For a scientist, the information in a journal article published in an impacted journal is not the same as the same information available in a teaching course because the process of the creation of each type of document is itself an indicator of quality. Thus, the mere fact that the journal article has undergone a review process is enough to confer on it more credibility than the other document typology. For this reason, specifying the source and typology of a document is almost more important than the relevance criteria.

Related to the above, academic search engines must reflect the existing research evaluation system and count with a citation extraction and processing system that aids the appreciation of the indexed items. Within science, the citation system is the main way of assessing the quality of a document and, by extension, the quality of researchers, journals or organizations as well. In this way, citation counting and the addition of bibliometric indicators are more than a recommended option, they are the key points around which a specialized database becomes an academic search engine. Further, it is recommended that these systems incorporate elaborate information elements derived from the data – such as charts, visualization devices and benchmarking tools – that enable the user to obtain a deep knowledge of the current scientific activity as well as to make the services more useful to research assessment. At the same time, the emergence of profiling services enhance this perspective because the analysis of aggregated data at an author and an organizational level favours their comparison and evaluation.

With regard to the actual searching, a specialized user needs advanced tools that enable the design of different search strategies and allow him/her to formulate data from the most precise queries to the most broad. A system which boasts of being an academic search engine should have an extensive and accurate index of the main items, a wide range of shortcuts and tips that enables the customization of queries, and a complete advanced search section that makes the clear retrieval of records effective. In addition, academic search engines must show transparency on the way in which the search system works and how the results are arranged. Since scientists are very demanding users, who use the results to find out about research and to locate other related works, it is essential that they know precisely what information is contained in a search engine and where the data come from. Thus, the users of academic search engines require that the result counts are not rounded off, that not merely a fraction of the results are visible, that the system shows non-retrievable items, and that the exporting of resulting records is limited. A scientific user is quite sensitive to these deficiencies and is distrustful of opaque systems where he/she is unaware of the origin and treatment of the retrieved information.

The evolution of academic search engines

In 1997, before the birth of Google and when AltaVista was the most-respected search engine, CiteSeer was born as a research project with the intention of becoming the first search engine devoted to scientific information accessible via the web (Figure 1.2). Using a web crawler and a parsing system, it gathered and indexed scholarly documents uploaded by researchers to their personal web pages or to the increasingly available repositories. But perhaps the most interesting feature of this project was that it made possible the automatic extraction and indexation of the references inserted into these documents, thereby counting citations which made it a research evaluation tool as well. CiteSeer could be said to be the starting point for these academic systems, because the introduction of an autonomous citation index marked a clear distinction between simple search engines that filtered academic information and a new specific searching tool designed by scientists for scientists.

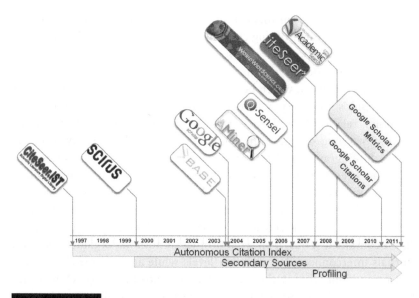

Figure 1.2   Timeline of academic search engines

Three years later, in 2000, Elsevier conceived of Scirus, an academic search engine with a difference. Even though it was based within web page crawling, this engine introduced a series of secondary authoritative sources that provided higher-quality contents and avoided having to parse the information because it was already processed. This contributed to records of a higher consistency and reliability, avoiding CiteSeer's main problem of data extracted directly from non-structured documents, causing many mistakes. The use of these sources evidenced the proliferation of new information resources on the web and the accession of scientific publishers' web platforms. These developments laid the foundations for future releases that increasingly will use secondary sources to support their systems.

But the academic search engine that would become a milestone was Google Scholar, created in 2004, because it combined web crawling through powerful bots with the use of authoritative sources which, by agreement, allowed data extraction from their sites. Moreover, it also incorporated its own autonomous citation index that enriched the relevance of the results. In this way, Google Scholar included the main characteristics of an academic search engine – web crawling, authoritative sources and citation indexing – but expanded them until it became the largest scientific information service with citation data.

The final landmark in this evolution of academic search engines was the emergence of the profiling concept and the design of academic search engines that incorporated elaborate information from the harvested data. The first attempt in this direction was AMiner (also known as ArnetMiner) in 2006, which before it became a search engine tried to be a researcher's directory where each profile was connected through co-author relationships. Hence, this social networking project became the first profiling service, although its data were taken mainly from the Digital Bibliography and Library Project (DBLP) and it was limited to computer science. But the first search engine that integrated the profiling concept akin to a real academic search engine was Microsoft Academic Search in 2009. Truly, this search solution was a structured engine that aggregated in different entities or objects the bibliographic information that it contained. Thus, it showed profiles of authors, organizations and journals interconnected at different levels while at the same time acting as a navigational tool. Other characteristics introduced by AMiner and Microsoft Academic Search included the use of visualization elements such as co-author networks and timeline charts which made available elaborated information from the gathered data as well as benchmarking tools that permitted comparison between research areas or organizations. This use of profiles and research evaluation tools initiated a revolutionary change, moving from simple search services of research documents to research assessment instruments that offered an aggregated view of the global research performance. This new environment roused Google, which launched Google Scholar Citations for author profiling in 2011 and Google Scholar Metrics for journal evaluation in 2012. Both of these applications are an attempt to counteract the successful Microsoft movement and to take up a stance for the future of academic search engines.

Future perspectives

Over the last few years, the appearance of new functionalities in academic search engines has paved the way for future developments that will influence the features of search engines and, by extension, the research activity assessment.

Perhaps the first expectation that these engines induced was that they would cover a wider document typology from a variety of sources. From a research evaluation point of view, this introduced a new perspective on research impact and production because scholarly activity was not only accessible for the purposes of research, but was now open to a broader range of activities such as teaching and popularization. In addition, the use of open access sources and small publishers' sites would produce a more complete map of research activity at a local and a national level and would highlight a new and comprehensive dimension on the research impact of certain disciplines, authors and organizations. The indexation of any scholarly document by Google Scholar was a revolutionary approach that shook the base of bibliometrics, highlighting a new and different notion of academic impact and production on the web (Aguillo, 2012).

On the other hand, however, the proliferation of profiling instruments has caused the focus of the research evaluation to fall, not only in journals, as was happening with traditional citation indexes, but also in other important elements involved in scientific production, such as authors and organizations. This has made possible the adoption of aggregated bibliometric indicators (the h-index) and the building of rankings that enhance the research evaluation at the producers' level. Thus, the pioneering impact of AMiner on authors and journals, and later Microsoft Academic Search on organizations, is welcomed as an initiative that addressed the improvement of the research evaluation and the scientometric study on the research activity at several levels. In the same way that citation indexes were the starting point for citation analyses, these new profiling products were a new encouragement to go in deep on collaboration relationships and the research impact in organizations.

But the most exciting possibility that these profiling services offer is that they pave the way for the implementation of Web 2.0 and social networking tools that make possible interaction between researchers when it comes to locating potential partners, sharing information and discussing research issues (Waldrop, 2008). The *follower* option of Google Scholar Citations or the *subscribe* option of Microsoft Academic Search are small initiatives, but they could spearhead more interactive tools such as chat rooms, forums, internal messaging, and so on, that assist social networking among scientists. In this way, altmetrics indicators would be introduced to measure profile views, paper downloads and follower numbers (Priem et al., 2011). This would add a 'societal' dimension to research activity, introducing concepts such as popularity and participation which are as important to research activity as the production or the impact.

2

CiteSeerˣ: a scientific engine for scientists

Abstract: In this chapter I describe the emergence of the first academic search engine based on its own crawling process and an autonomous citation index. CiteSeerˣ is also depicted as an experimental instrument arising from scientific research within the scientific community, and a potential host of future developments. Its principal problem resides in a poor parsing technology that affects the identification of the principal elements of a research document. This weakness also influences the citation extraction and count, a critical aspect of the research evaluation. The chapter concludes by suggesting that this service has lost strength and appears to be at something of a standstill in terms of both its functioning and its coverage.

Key words: CiteSeerˣ, autonomous citation index, digital library, parsing.

In 1997 the first academic search engine, CiteSeer (*http://citeseerx.ist. psu.edu*), was born, understood to be the first web-based search engine specializing in scientific information. It was developed at the NEC Research Institute in Princeton, by Steve Lawrence, Lee Giles and Kurt Bollacker. In 2003 it was moved to Pennsylvania State University's College of Information Sciences and Technology, where Lee Giles now manages the project. In 2008, CiteSeer became CiteSeerˣ, a new implementation based on a new architecture and data model which intended to improve on previous technical weaknesses and present a new product according to the new needs of the scientific community (CiteSeerˣ, 2013a). Unlike other search engines, CiteSeerˣ is characterized as being an open and non-profit service which makes its data accessible in order to support other research projects.

The principal characteristic of this search engine which makes it unique to other products is that it shows an eminent scientific origin, designed by researchers and hosted by a university faculty. In this way, CiteSeer[x] is not presented as just another specialized search engine, but as the applied result of the research developed by the Giles team in the field of information retrieval and search engineering. This means that Citeseer[x] is not seen as a business product designed to compete in a commercial way, but as an advanced prototype in the vanguard of future developments in the academic search engine world. However, although CiteSeer[x] can be considered to be a pioneer in academic searching, at the present time it has lost the initiative and has not been able to keep pace with recent developments in the market. CiteSeer[x] is a product designed by scientists for scientists and its most important contribution to the academic searching environment was the development of automated citation indexing, allowing the creation of an autonomous citation index. With this technical innovation, CiteSeer[x] introduced an assessment tool that marked the birth of academic search engines and the possibility of the bibliometric evaluation of web papers.

Another feature of this search engine is that really it acts like a digital library. Unlike other search engines, which extract text information and metadata from the crawled pages, CiteSeer[x] is only formed of free and open-accessed scientific documents on the web. The formats used to identify these documents are PDF, PS and other compression formats such as ZIP or GZIP. CiteSeer[x] automatically deposits a copy of these documents, making it possible to download the original document not from its actual location but from the CiteSeer[x] repository.

Autonomous citation indexing

As stated above, CiteSeer[x] was conceived as a research product, born from a research project and created by scientists for scientists. This 'meta' academic dimension meant that CiteSeer[x] could implement a citation indexing system that would make possible the evaluation of the harvested documents not only for their relevance but for their scientific impact as well. Unlike traditional citation databases such as Web of Science, in which the citation index is manually built, CiteSeer[x] led with a novel and completely self-sufficient citation indexing process. This system shows the advantage of reflecting an earlier view of a paper's impact because citations are calculated when the paper is available on the web, independent of journal publication delays. Another benefit is that it operates in a completely independent way, without human intervention, reducing the system's economic and time costs. Furthermore, CiteSeer^x can extract the citation context to understand the reasoning and sense of a citation in a paper (Giles et al., 1998). In short, the principal conceptual contribution of CiteSeer^x is that it takes the article's focus as the basic research unit, moving the journal concept to a secondary place.

The procedure to automatically obtain citations is as follows: CiteSeer^x crawls the web looking for documents in PDF, PS and ZIP formats. These files are downloaded to its digital library and the metadata about the document are added to its tables. Next, they are converted to text to parse the content and to extract the citations embedded within the context in which the citations are made, indexing only the first 500 words of each document. Finally, this information is stored in a database. Because a reference can be presented in different formats, such as APA, Harvard or Chicago style, CiteSeer^x uses algorithms for identifying and grouping variations of the same reference, making it possible to count the number of citations that a paper receives. These citations are bridges that connect one paper to another, which makes it possible to browse CiteSeer^x's content, jumping between cited papers (Stribling et al., 2006).

A focus on computer science

The only reference to the the search engine's coverage is in the 'History' section of CiteSeer^x. There, it is claimed that, 'Since its inception, the original CiteSeer grew to index over 750,000 documents ...', the moment at which CiteSeer became CiteSeer^x (CiteSeer^x, 2013a). Today, looking for a neutral term 'a', it retrieves almost four times more documents, approximately 2.8 million, and presents 5.1 million citations extracted from those documents (in February 2014). This amount is far more than earlier crawls that reported 1.6 million documents (Teregowda et al., 2010; Fiala, 2011), although there are three years between the two observations. However, the most reliable figure is that made available by BASE, an academic search engine which integrated CiteSeer^x's records at the end of 2013. According to BASE, CiteSeer^x contains 3.3 million documents. Similarly, searching in the author index, it is estimated that it contains approximately 310,000 identified authors, although the proportion of duplicated profiles is quite high (10.4 per cent). CiteSeer^x

does not allow us to distinguish the document by type of file nor by subject class, therefore it is difficult to extract further information on how the documents are distributed within the search engine. I have only been able to obtain data about the publication date distribution of the records: 1,488,000 documents (52.5 per cent) were retrieved asking for the publication date in the advanced search. This percentage is rather low and shows that almost half of the records have no date or cannot be retrieved by the system. Moreover, a manual inspection of historical records from 1900 to 1970 shows inaccurate dates in the majority of cases, due to page number confusion. In Figure 2.1 it can be seen that the highest number of records corresponds to the periods 2005–9 (28.7 per cent) and 2000–2004 (27.9 per cent) while the most recent period, 2009–13, represents only 12.5 per cent. It is also interesting to note the little notch in 2006, which suggests data lost when the search engine altered its architecture and changed from CiteSeer to CiteSeer^x. This may be interpreted as a symptom of poor updating and a certain listlessness in maintaining a competitive product. This data loss could also be due to a scalability problem, whereby the system cannot enlarge the database because it does not have enough technical resources. This would explain the birth of CiteSeer^x in 2008.

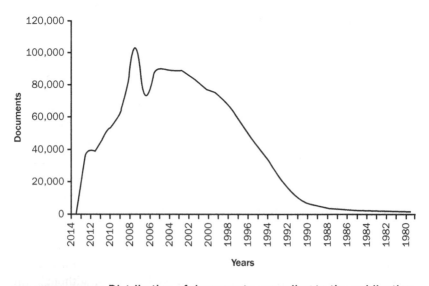

Figure 2.1 Distribution of documents according to the publication date in CiteSeer^x

As to the rest of its content, CiteSeer^x does not make explicit the thematic coverage of the indexed documents and does not appear to be a specialized search engine, rather a generalist one. However, a brief exploration of the service allows us to suggest that most of the documents come from the field of computer science. Moreover, in certain sections, such as MyCiteSeer^x, it is clearly stated that 'MyCiteSeer^x is a personal content portal for the CiteSeer^x, a scientific literature digital library and search engine that focuses primarily on the literature in computer and information science' (CiteSeer^x, 2013c). And in the 'Most Cited' lists, computer science is always mentioned as the discipline of these rankings. These facts allow us to claim that CiteSeer^x really is a specialized computing and information science search engine, although it does host documents from other disciplines as well.

A searchable digital library

Unlike other search engines, retrieved records in the results page do not give direct access to the referenced resource but to a bibliographic record with detailed information about the document and its citation context (see Figure 2.2). This is because CiteSeer^x is also a digital library that stores documents that it locates on the web. Each record contains, firstly, information that identifies the file, such as title, publication year, author, venue and number of citations from CiteSeer^x. Secondly, on the left side, a box is presented that displays several functions describing what users can do with the record, such as: save it; add it to any personal collections; suggest any corrections and monitor the changes in the record. In this way, CiteSeer^x promotes interaction with its users to improve its bibliographic database, perhaps due to the multiple failures of its parsing system, as we will see below (see p. 20). The left-side margin shows the access to the document copies ('Cached') hosted in the search engine and the list of URLs ('Download links') from where the search engine located the file. These addresses correspond in most cases to repositories, university domains or personal homepages where these documents are freely available on the web. Halfway down the figure, five tabs provide detailed information about the file:

- 'Summary' presents an abstract extracted from the paper and a list of 'citations'. This introduces an element of confusion between the citations given in the top left of the figure (the number of times that the paper is cited) and the list of citations in this summary section (the list of references cited by the paper). This list only shows the references of indexed papers in CiteSeer^x – including, to the left of the reference, the number of citations each paper has received – ignoring all other references.

On the right-hand side of the record there are two boxes. The 'BibTeX' box restates the information that identifies the document, but does so now in BibTeX format. BibTeX is an extended reference manager software that was developed for documents in LaTeX format and PostScript documents. This format is supported by a wide variety of reference manager tools and makes it possible to export references from CiteSeer^x to other bibliographical software. However, it is surprising that the information in BibTeX is more detailed than that presented in the records. For example, in Figure 2.2 the BibTeX template contains volume and page numbers – important data for the location and identification of a document – which CiteSeer^x omits in its record page.

The second box, 'Years of Citing Articles', details in a longitudinal graph the publication date of the papers that cite the document. This is a very interesting and original feature that indicates the currency of the article, whether it is a classical work or even a 'sleeping beauty' (Van Raan, 2004).

- 'Active Bibliography' gathers together the papers indexed in CiteSeer^x that cite the particular document, along with the number of citations that these papers receive.

- 'Co-citation' displays papers that are also cited together with the particular document. This tab, along with Active Bibliography tab, allows the user to search according to the citation context of the document to find relevant documents. The number of citations in both tabs makes it possible to select the most valuable documents according to their scientific impact.

- 'Clustered Documents' contains the different versions of the document housed by the search engine. This shows that CiteSeer^x handles duplicated records well, and can store in one record an identical document from different sources.

- 'Version History' highlights which data were extracted from each clustered document and which source was used. Thus, citations are parsed with ParsCit and the text information is parsed with SVM HeaderParse. While this information is relevant for the maintenance of the database, it is less relevant for users.

Figure 2.2 Record page of an indexed document in CiteSeer^x (17 February 2014)

Another interesting section is the 'Most Cited: Documents, Citations, Authors and Venue Impact Rating' on the home page. This provides distinct rankings of items by citations. The documents and citations rankings can be complete (for all years) or limited by year from 1990 to 2013. Unlike document ranking, the citations ranking contains the most-cited documents not included in CiteSeer^x. However, the number of citations provided does not match the total amount presented in the document page due to the variable updating rates between the lists and the general database, a fact that is noted in each ranking. At the time of writing, the 'Venue Impact Rating' was not working, so I cannot discuss what information it contains nor what its validity is.

Searching for authors and citations

CiteSeer^x runs its searches in Apache Solr, an open access search platform developed by Apache Lucene. It shows versatility in the handling of rich files (Word, PDF, and so on) and is highly scalable for web search engines. It also offers three search plugins – general search, author search and title search – for web browsers that support the OpenSearch specification. CiteSeer^x presents the standard appearance of a search engine with only a text box to launch queries. As a reminder that it is a web citation database, it also includes a check to search citations within the indexed documents. These citations correspond to the bibliographic references extracted from the indexed documents, although many of these citations point to non-indexed documents. CiteSeer^x also includes an advanced search page but its possibilities are rather limited. It enables the user to search in seven metadata fields that describe each record: Text, Title, Author Name, Author Affiliation, Publication Venue, Key Words and Abstract (CiteSeer^x, 2013b). These tips support wildcards, double quotes for exact phrases and Booleans queries. However, the tips don't really search into the metadata content of each record, but into a different index in which some erroneous tags are removed, avoiding the retrieval of inaccurate records. For example, numerous records were observed for which the author is listed as 'unknown authors'. Upon attempting to find out how many records present this failure (`author: "unknown authors"`) the system returned that this search did not match any documents. The same happens when searching for documents with no publication year or no title – the metadata field simply disappears from the records and is not retrievable. A previous study also found that queries that used a sentence with double quotes did not retrieve the exact sentence but retrieved one employing similar wording and terminology (Reeve, 2005). 'Range Criteria' allows the user to delimit the search by publication date and define the 'Minimum Number of Citations' to retrieve the most-cited documents. As a general search, this makes it possible to mark the inclusion of citations. Finally, the 'Sorting Criteria' present the retrieved results in five ways, by: citations, relevance, date (descending), date (ascending) and recency. This last criterion sorts the results by thematic relevance and by the newness of the records, thus preventing relevant but obsolete documents assuming the highest rankings (Dong et al., 2010).

The results page displays the retrieved records in lists of ten, something which cannot be changed (see Figure 2.3). This means that browsing the pages is tedious and slow. Another – perhaps more important – problem is that it is only possible to view the first 500 records in each query. This reduces its value because it is not possible to know exactly how many records are retrieved in a query, and it hinders performing exhaustive queries. However, if you are registered with CiteSeer^x you can export the

Documents   Authors   Tables   MetaCart   Sign up   Log in

CiteSeer[x]$_\beta$

☐ Include Citations   Advanced Search   Search

Results 1 - 10 of 2,833,130   Next 10 →   Tools

Functions from a set to a set
by Czesław Byliński - *Journal of Formalized Mathematics*, 1989
"... Science, Univ. of Bialystok Functions from a Set to a Set Czesław Byliński Warsaw University Bialystok ..."
Abstract - Cited by 1007 (23 self) - Add to MetaCart

Sorted by:
Relevance ▼

Try your query at
Scholar   Yahoo!   Ask
Bing   CSB   Libra

A Framework for Defining Logics
by Robert Harper, Furio Honsell, Gordon Plotkin - *JOURNAL OF THE ASSOCIATION FOR COMPUTING MACHINERY*, 1993
"... A Framework for Defining Logics Robert Harper Furio Honsell y Gordon Plotkin z Abstract ..."
Abstract - Cited by 696 (39 self) - Add to MetaCart

A theory of timed automata
by Rajeev Alur, 1999
"... Timed Automata Rajeev Alur ∗ Abstract. Model checking is emerging as a practical tool ..."
Abstract - Cited by 1975 (31 self) - Add to MetaCart

Reinforcement learning: a survey
by Leslie Pack Kaelbling, Michael L. Littman, Andrew W. Moore - *Journal of Artificial Intelligence Research*, 1996
"... /96 Reinforcement Learning: A Survey Leslie Pack Kaelbling lpk@(email omitted); Michael L. Littman mlittman ..."
Abstract - Cited by 1298 (23 self) - Add to MetaCart

Data Clustering: A Review
by A.K Jain, M N Murty, P. J. Flynn - *ACM COMPUTING SURVEYS*, 1999
"... Data Clustering: A Review A.K. JAIN Michigan State University M.N. MURTY Indian Institute ..."
Abstract - Cited by 1284 (13 self) - Add to MetaCart

Figure 2.3 Screenshot of the results page of CiteSeer[x] (17 February 2014)

results, which makes it possible to analyse them offline and assess their relevance. To a great extent, this enhances the use of CiteSeer[x] for bibliometric or other data analysis purposes. At this stage, the page shows links to the most important generalist and specialized search engines – such as Google Scholar, Bing, Yahoo! or Libra (Microsoft Academic Search since 2009) – to widen the query.

CiteSeer[x] also incorporates an author index that lets the user retrieve the names of those responsible for the indexed documents. This index groups the different variants of author names into a standard list, taking into account the similar collection of metadata from papers of authors with similar names (Huang et al., 2006). Each author result shows the name, name variants, affiliations, number of papers and, in some cases, a personal homepage. Each author result also provides access to more detailed information on the person, with a list of his/her publications and the h-index as a bibliometric indicator. But perhaps one of the most valuable characteristics is that the data can be edited and modified – merging similar names in the same profile, removing or adding publications to the list, and correcting names and affiliations. This makes the author search more consistent and reliable.

So, CiteSeer[x] enables the user to search in a novel table index which contains a list of tables extracted from the parsed documents. The table results page shows the table caption, the title of the document, the author and date, and a portion of text where the table is mentioned. However, in my opinion, although this is an original table index its usefulness is limited because the information can be indexed into the general document search. Further, this type of data does not have sufficient depth to require its own index. Perhaps a citation or figure index would be more useful.

Parsing mistakes

One of the most important failures of CiteSeer[x] lies in its parsing of citations and documents. The search engine still makes mistakes when extracting basic data from each document – such as incomplete citations and incorrect dates and titles. CiteSeer[x] uses ParsCit to extract citations from documents (Councill et al., 2008), an open access project that addresses citation extraction and the definition of references' structures. However, the process of obtaining references from the bibliography and displaying them in the results page contains important weaknesses. For example, Figure 2.4 presents a results page with citations; beside each citation a box contains the actual reference taken from one of the documents that includes that citation. The first citation shows that the name of the second author, Hassenblatt, is included in the title, as does the fourth citation with the author Yuan. This same fourth citation presents the publication date as 2000, whereas the reference is actually from 1995. In addition, relevant information is also missing, as in the case of the first citation which omits the publication source, making it impossible to know if it is a journal paper or a book chapter. Similarly, the second citation does not contain the publisher's name (Cambridge University Press). Further, I have also seen that some citations are not given in the citing documents, although I have not been able to quantify how many miscounts exist. I have indeed observed that the counting of citations varies according to the way in which the records are presented in the database. Thus, the citations in the results page can be different from the citations in the record page and when the list of citing papers is explored (see Figure 2.5). These mistakes and instances of missing

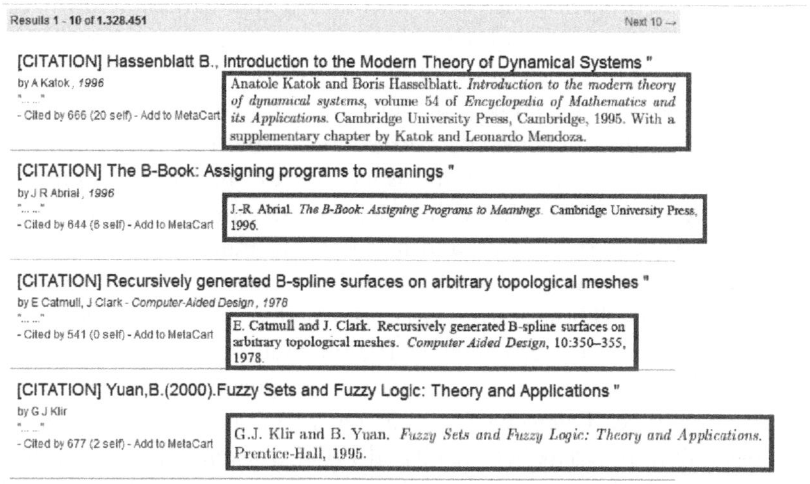

[CITATION] Hassenblatt B., Introduction to the Modern Theory of Dynamical Systems "

by A Katok , 1996

"... "

- Cited by 666 (20 self) - Add to MetaCart

> Anatole Katok and Boris Hasselblatt. *Introduction to the modern theory of dynamical systems*, volume 54 of *Encyclopedia of Mathematics and its Applications*. Cambridge University Press, Cambridge, 1995. With a supplementary chapter by Katok and Leonardo Mendoza.

[CITATION] The B-Book: Assigning programs to meanings "

by J R Abrial , 1996

"... "

- Cited by 644 (8 self) - Add to MetaCart

> J.-R. Abrial. *The B-Book: Assigning Programs to Meanings*. Cambridge University Press, 1996.

[CITATION] Recursively generated B-spline surfaces on arbitrary topological meshes "

by E Catmull, J Clark - *Computer-Aided Design* , 1978

- Cited by 541 (0 self) - Add to MetaCart

> E. Catmull and J. Clark. Recursively generated B-spline surfaces on arbitrary topological meshes. *Computer Aided Design*, 10:350–355, 1978.

[CITATION] Yuan,B.(2000).Fuzzy Sets and Fuzzy Logic: Theory and Applications "

by G J Klir

- Cited by 677 (2 self) - Add to MetaCart

> G.J. Klir and B. Yuan. *Fuzzy Sets and Fuzzy Logic: Theory and Applications*. Prentice-Hall, 1995.

Figure 2.4 Detailed view of how citations are presented in CiteSeer^x and how they are inserted into an indexed document

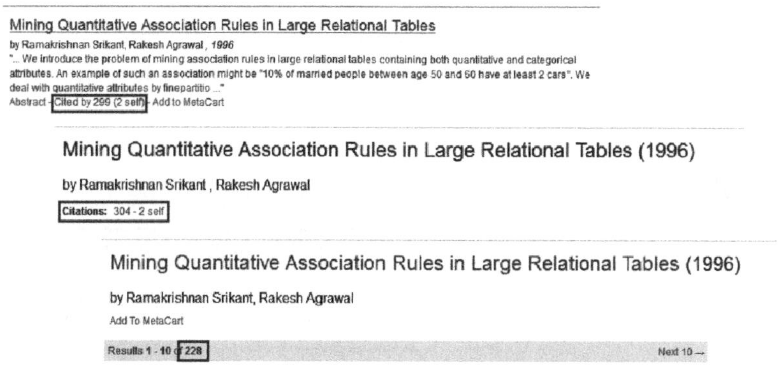

Mining Quantitative Association Rules In Large Relational Tables

by Ramakrishnan Srikant, Rakesh Agrawal , 1996

"... We introduce the problem of mining association rules in large relational tables containing both quantitative and categorical attributes. An example of such an association might be "10% of married people between age 50 and 60 have at least 2 cars". We deal with quantitative attributes by fineparititio ..."

Abstract - Cited by 299 (2 self) - Add to MetaCart

Mining Quantitative Association Rules in Large Relational Tables (1996)

by Ramakrishnan Srikant , Rakesh Agrawal

Citations: 304 - 2 self

Mining Quantitative Association Rules in Large Relational Tables (1996)

by Ramakrishnan Srikant, Rakesh Agrawal

Add To MetaCart

Results 1 - 10 of 228   Next 10 →

Figure 2.5 Several views of citation miscounting for the same document in CiteSeer^x

information can throw serious doubts on the validity of the citation counts and their use for bibliometric citation analyses. Chen et al. (2006), in a study on the CiteSeer metadata, also pointed out that missing or incorrectly parsed references are enough to undermine the validity of citation analyses from these data.

These same problems with citation counting and extraction have been detected in the processing of text information such as abstracts and titles (Nie et al., 2007a). This task is performed with SVM HeaderParse. Figure 2.6 shows two examples in which the extracted abstract processed by the parser does not exactly correspond to the real abstract of the documents – cutting text and displaying an incomplete summary. Something similar happens with article titles, some of which are not captured in the correct form, and it is not uncommon to find spurious and inexact titles such as 'unknown title', 'title', 'contents' and other unusual forms. These errors were estimated when searching for document titles and approximately 19,000 confusing headlines (1.3 per cent) were found, which is a significant proportion. In terms of the publication date, I detected 52,000 items (3.5 percent) presenting a strange publication date between 0 and 1900. One might think that these dates correspond to ancient digitalized documents, as will be seen with Scirus, but actually they all belong to documents published later than 1900 for which the parser has confused the publication date with the pagination, series number, volume, etc. (see Figure 2.7). Further, the

Functions from a set to a set (1989)

by Czesław Byliński

Venue: Journal of Formalized Mathematics
Citations: 991 - 23 self

Abstract
function from a set X into a set Y, denoted by "Function of X,Y ", the set of all functions from a set X into a set Y, denoted by Funcs(X,Y), and the permutation of a set (mode Permutation of X, where X is a set). Theorems and schemes included in the article are reformulations of the theorems of [1] in the new terminology. Also some basic facts about functions of two variables are proved.

> **Summary.** The article is a continuation of [1]. We define the following concepts: a function from a set X into a set Y, denoted by "Function of X,Y", the set of all functions from a set X into a set Y, denoted by Funcs(X,Y), and the permutation of a set (mode Permutation of X, where X is a set). Theorems and schemes included in the article are reformulations of the theorems of [1] in the new terminology. Also some basic facts about functions of two variables are proved.

The ubiquitous B-tree (1979)

by Douglas Comer

Venue: ACM Computing Surveys
Citations: 501 - 0 self

Abstract
B-trees have become, de facto, a standard for file organization. File indexes of users, dedicated database systems, and general-purpose access methods have all been proposed and implemented using B-trees This paper reviews B-trees and shows why they have been so successful It discusses the major variations of the B-tree, especially the B+-tree.

> B-trees have become, de facto, a standard for file organization. File indexes of users, dedicated database systems, and general-purpose access methods have all been proposed and implemented using B-trees This paper reviews B-trees and shows why they have been so successful It discusses the major variations of the B-tree, especially the B+-tree, contrasting the relative merits and costs of each implementation. It illustrates a general purpose access method which uses a B-tree.

Figure 2.6 Comparison between extracted abstracts in CiteSeer[x] and the actual abstracts from each document

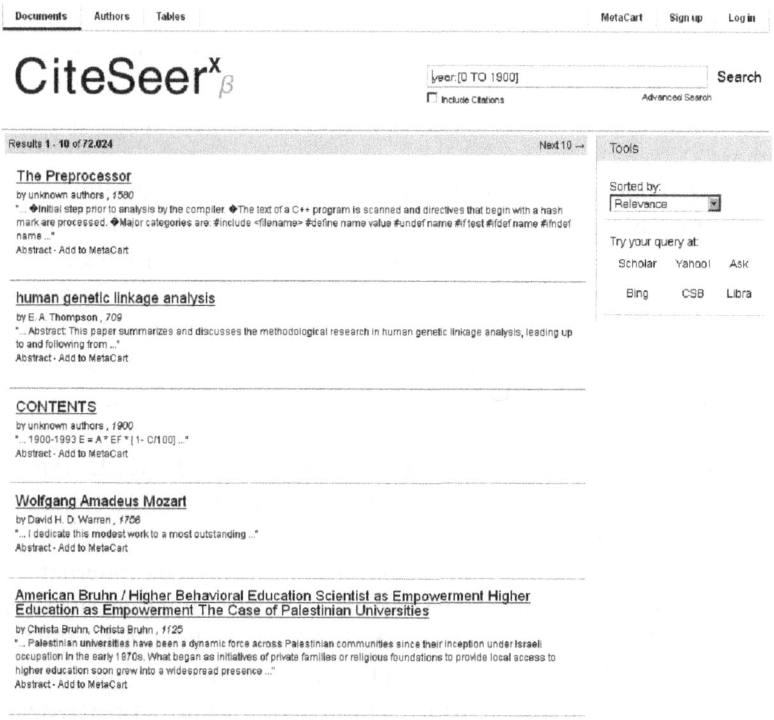

Figure 2.7 Results page from the query: documents published between 0 and 1900 (17 February 2014)

aforementioned problems on the absence of the indexation of erroneous data suggest that these failures may be more numerous than just those observed. A crawl was carried out to obtain information on these non-retrievable mistakes and to make an estimation of the size of the problem. I automatically crawled 150,000 document pages randomly selected using an SQL script during February 2014. From the data, it was detected that 14.2 per cent were removed documents. That is, these documents are included in the searchable index but they are removed from the database. Of the active documents, only 1.6 per cent do not show any title. A further 45 per cent do not display information on publication year, which, along with the 3.5 per cent of erroneous publication years, adds up to almost 49 per cent of irregular publication dates. A similar scenario was found with venue data, for which 32.6 per cent of the results contained no publication source. From a bibliometric perspective, only 48.5 per cent of the records were cited, although it is not known if these are only the citations that CiteSeer^x's parser is able to extract. In terms of author information, only 36.7 per cent of papers in CiteSeer^x are assigned to an author, while the rest are not identified by the author index. These comprise the aforementioned 'unknown authors'.

Another important problem is that there is no standardization in the presentation of authors, journal titles and affiliations, so these can be presented in a very diverse way. These inconsistencies arise because the textual parser takes the information from the source as it is and the system does not do anything to make the entries uniform. For author names this problem can be solved because CiteSeer^x has an independent author index in which it groups similar authors from similar institutions – this list can then be edited to correct mistakes. This is not the case for venue source information however. To take the SIGMOD (Special Interest Group on Management of Data) of the ACM (Association for Computing Machinery) conferences as an example, up to eight variants of the same conference were found (ACM SIGMOD International Conference on Management of Data, In ACM SIGMOD, In SIGMOD, SIGMOD RECORD, Proceedings of SIGMOD, In Proc. SIGMOD, In SIGMOD. ACM, In SIGMOD Conference), which does not preclude there being more variations. More serious problems are associated with affiliations because even though there is a tip to search in the affiliations field (*affil:*), it is not possible to know if the obtained results correspond to the launched query because the returned records do not have an affiliation field.

Other 'Seers': the CiteSeer^x lab

As we have seen above, CiteSeer^x is not only an academic search engine but it is also a scientific platform through which the developers of the engine test new products or prototypes that improve CiteSeer^x itself and offer new solutions to information science in general. As a web laboratory, the CiteSeer^x repository is also used to test these developments (Bhatia et al., 2012). Four 'Seers' are at the disposal of users checking the new creations. These 'Seers' were accessible from the homepage until December 2013 but are now linked from the research group's web page:

- *RefSeer* is an automatic advising service that recommends the most appropriate bibliographic references in CiteSeer^x according to the text of an abstract or a full document (He et al., 2010). It returns several topics identified from the text and lists the most cited document in each topic group. Each reference shows the title, authors, a brief summary and a citation count. Surprisingly, these citations do not tally with the other citation counts of CiteSeer^x. This tool is new and interesting because it can enhance the writing of a piece of research by suggesting new references that would enrich the text. However, I think that selecting important references for a study is a complex task that goes beyond text processing. It implies a deep knowledge of a discipline, its relevant sources and authors, and a complete understanding of the references. Therefore, I consider that the utility of this functionality is suitable for broadening knowledge, but rather less so when it comes to inclusion in a bibliography.

- *AckSeer* is a development that indexes the acknowledgements that authors include in their papers, expressing thanks for support received from funding agencies or other types of grants, and showing gratitude to anonymous referees (Khabsa et al., 2012). This application identifies the entities, both organizational and individual, which are mentioned in the acknowledgements. According to the 'About' page (AckSeer, 2014a), AckSeer extracts these data from more than 500,000 documents indexed in CiteSeer^x, obtaining four million entities of which two million are unique. AlchemyAPI and OpenCalais are used to extract these entities. A 'Statistics' page (AckSeer, 2014b) displays a pie chart on which the most numerous entities are Persons (63.5 per cent), Organizations (27.3 per cent) and Companies (9.2 per cent). The results page shows the acknowledgements that correspond to the queried entity. These are sorted by citations and present the document title, the acknowledgement text and the entities that were indexed from each document. It is interesting to view the timeline option because this shows a longitudinal graph where the user can see the number of times that a person or organization is mentioned in acknowledgements each year. However – and as is the case with the CiteSeer^x main project – there is no standardization nor cleaning process, meaning that entities are presented in different forms, which leads to long and complex queries to retrieve the acknowledgements to one specific organization. So, although this tool is of limited use to information science, from a scientometric perspective the information is of great value in terms of knowing who is funding scientific activity, who are the most prestigious researchers in terms of article reviews and feedback, and how the support of an organization to certain projects evolves over time.

- *CollabSeer* recommends possible partners from the co-authors network and the most usual research topics for a given researcher. It works by vectoring the number of co-authors of an individual author's personal network; next, the similarity between the network structure of two authors is calculated; and, finally, the system ranks authors by similarity, suggesting that authors with similar partners are potential collaborators (Chen et al., 2011). This is complemented with an analysis of both authors' most relevant shared terms. Similarity is computed using three extended and popular similarity measures: the Jaccard index, cosine, and topology overlapping. From an author query, CollabSeer returns a list of possible authors and their affiliations. Each author's page shows its co-authors and a list of suggested collaborators which can be ranked according to the three similarity measures. This project is based on the general assumption in social network analysis that two people who are connected with the same partners increase their likelihood of establishing a tie between them (structural holes) (Burt, 1992). However, and as with RefSeer, this tool is of limited use because the search for possible collaborators is a complex task that depends on the projects that a researcher wishes to develop, their personal contacts and the viability of this collaboration in terms of geographical distance, economic resources, etc. Perhaps, from a scientometric point of view, this application can help indicate the probability of one author collaborating with another one and hence forecast scientific dynamics, but I have doubts about the usefulness of CollabSeer in searching for future partners.

- *SeerSeer* is an experimental development authored by Pucktada Treeratpituk, a member of the CiteSeer[x] research team. Based on the CiteSeer[x] digital library, it acts as a search engine to locate experts in certain knowledge areas (although the majority of the documents come from the field of computer science). SeerSeer allows the user to search directly by authors or by research disciplines. The author search retrieves a personal profile of an author with basic bibliometric information (publication year, publication count, citation count and h-index), a flow map highlighting how some topics come from other concepts, a timeline that shows the evolution of the main research key words, and, finally, a list of his/her papers in CiteSeer[x]. This author profile is interesting because it provides a detailed analysis of the research topics on which an author is working, but the inconsistency in the key words selection is less satisfactory. The research discipline search returns the most relevant authors in the queried research area, ranked by citations and with a topic cloud representative of that discipline.

A pioneer in citation indexing

As was said at the beginning of this chapter, CiteSeer^x has to be understood as a research development, the main propose of which is to put in practice the new advances achieved by the CiteSeer^x research team headed by Lee Giles. CiteSeer^x was the first search engine that could extract, process and index citations from scientific documents hosted on the web, and it maintained an automatic system that enabled it to expand and evolve to the present day. Without a doubt, this successful development was the seed for future academic search engines based on citations counts. However, the instability of the project – moving from different organizations and from person to person – and the development of different technical versions that could enable the continuity of the search engine have caused a certain lassitude of service and a lack of energy both in the reliability of the data and the consistency of parsed documents. The bell-shape of Figure 2.1 is symptomatic of the fact that the search engine has not evolved in the best way, and the size of its database – with only 3.3 million documents – indicates that CiteSeer^x has lost some of its force as a competitor in the academic search engine market. This fact was evidenced by Stribling et al. (2006), who noticed that service was not maintained after starting development at NEC.

Perhaps one of its most significant failures – and that most visible to the users – lay in the problem of parsing the information from each document. In the data consistency section above (p. 20), we saw that these errors were present in every type of extracted data. Thus, mistakes were found in abstracts, titles, names, publication years, etc. This creates a poor impression for users, and indicates that there is no cleaning process. In fact, its principal functionality – autonomous citation indexing – shows serious deficiencies because the citation count differs from one view of the (same) document to another. All of this advises against the use of CiteSeer^x for bibliometric studies and throws doubt on the citation values and rankings produced by the search engine. This could be the reason why bibliometric analyses from CiteSeer^x are few in number (Fiala, 2011). As we will see with other autonomous citation indexing systems, their principal drawback is that developments often led to a loss of consistency in the parsing process, and they needed to develop well-defined cleaning processes that solved the malfunctions of these automatic systems. In the case of CiteSeer^x, this cleaning process was absent, or it was left to the users to correct the mistakes.

3

Scirus: a multi-source searcher

Abstract: This chapter is devoted to the now-retired search engine, Scirus. Introduced by Elsevier in 2000 it was the first academic search engine that mixed up authoritative sources such as publisher platforms and open access repositories with a deep crawl of academic web pages. It also presented a complete search interface with an advanced filtering system that allowed the user to analyse their most relevant sources and their indexing problems. Its principal weaknesses were its poor duplication control – producing several entries for the same document or webpage, and its classification inconsistencies – producing many materials without a subject matter. The chapter concludes that Scirus is a significant loss for the academic community and a symptom of the instability of this market.

Key words: Scirus, Elsevier, academic web crawling, preferred web sources, search filtering.

On 2 February 2000, Elsevier, the giant of the scientific publishing world, launched the most comprehensive academic search engine of its time. Scirus, named after a mythological character of Ancient Greece with prophetic properties, supplied a varied range of scientific resources from web pages to peer-reviewed articles, patents, pre-prints and reports accessible via the web. Perhaps this was the principal difference of Scirus compared to other academic search engines: it was not only fed by several authoritative sources, but it also contained an important crawl of web pages from university and scientific websites. Thus, Scirus acted as a true specialized web search engine in which the user could retrieve web pages from research institutions. A web page was defined as an academic resource because it was hosted on a research site, rather than because of the actual content of the page. From an academic perspective this would generate some doubts as to the relevance of the pages. Perhaps because of this limitation Scirus was the first search engine to include a large and varied range of authoritative sources such as publisher portals, open repositories and specialized databases. But, unlike other academic search engines, Scirus was transparent about the origin of its data. Further, it was one of the few that made possible the retrieval of documents according to the sources.

However, in January 2014 Scirus closed its doors, and it is now impossible to use its search services anymore. The reason put forward for this cessation of activity was a loss of competitive edge against other platforms (Elsevier, 2013), which could indicate the changing world of the search engine and the strength of the latest developments in this sector. So, Elsevier withdraws from the web, focusing on its traditional scientific database, Scopus (Scopus, 2014a). Thus, this chapter describes the status of Scirus in August 2013 – the last time that the service was analysed.

Web pages and authoritative sources

As outlined above, Scirus contained a heterogeneous mix of documents and sources that could cause some confusion when searching. But at the same time it allowed the appreciation of a document by its origin. Scirus's homepage stated that it included more than 575 million scientific items, but this only corresponded to web pages. These constituted the core of the search engine, comprising 86.8 per cent of all the documents indexed by the search engine. The rest came from other bibliographic sources, making a total of approximately 662 million documents (see Figure 3.1). According to the 'About us' page (Scirus, 2013a), the web pages were mostly harvested from university web domains (71.5 per cent), while the remaining websites were distributed among organizations (10.4 per cent), companies (9.4 per cent) and government sites (8.7 per cent) (Table 3.1). However, this distribution did not give a precise definition of the web sources because national domains were not specified and top-level domains only corresponded with the American web. Thus, one had to suppose that the rest of the world's university sites were included in the 'Other STM and academic sites' category due to the very high number of sources in this section. This is supported by Ortega and Aguillo (2009), who noted a similar proportion of American academic web domains (36.9 per cent) compared to the rest of the world.

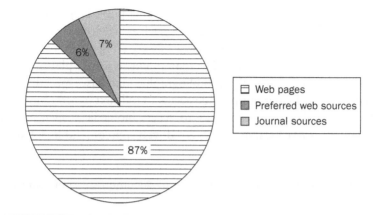

7%
6%

☐ Web pages
■ Preferred web sources
▨ Journal sources

87%

Figure 3.1   Contents distribution by source origin

Table 3.1   Distribution of web pages indexed by Scirus by web domain

Domain	Web pages	Distribution (%)
.edu	232,000,000	40.35
.org	60,000,000	10.43
.ac.uk	35,000,000	6.09
.com	54,000,000	9.39
.gov	50,000,000	8.70
Other STM and academic sites	144,000,000	25.04
Total	575,000,000	100.00

In addition to this huge number of web pages, Scirus also included a group of outstanding web resources which did not merely include web pages but also elaborated scientific documents such as research articles, pre-prints, reports or patent records. Perhaps these selected sites compensated for the heterogeneous and imprecise group of web pages. These additional web resources accounted for only 13.2 per cent (87.3 million documents) of the entire search engine and were divided among 'Journal sources' (7.5 per cent, or 49.8 million documents) and 'Preferred web sources' (5.6 per cent, or 37.5 million documents).

'Journal sources' corresponded to the online publishing platforms of the world's principal scientific publishers, such as ScienceDirect (Elsevier), SpringerLink (Springer) or Wiley Online Library (Wiley), although it also included information services other than publishers' web platforms. For example, PubMed is simply a bibliographic database specializing in biomedicine which does not provide access to full-text papers. Moreover, PubMed Central is a web gateway to access biomedical open journals that could be better located in 'Preferred web sources'. Table 3.2 shows

Table 3.2	Distribution of number of documents by publisher in 'Journal sources' section

Publisher	Documents	Distribution (%)	Document type
PubMed	22,300,000	44.72	Citations
ScienceDirect	11,600,000	23.26	Articles references
Springer	3,500,000	7.02	Articles references
PubMed Central	2,500,000	5.01	Full-text articles
Wiley-Blackwell	2,300,000	4.61	Articles references
Lippincott Williams & Wilkins	1,200,000	2.41	Articles references
Oxford University Press	935,000	1.88	Articles references
SAGE Publications	870,000	1.74	Articles references
Cambridge University Press	796,000	1.60	Articles references
Nature Publishing Group	767,000	1.54	Articles references
BMJ	686,000	1.38	Articles references
Scitation	558,000	1.12	Articles references
American Physical Society	528,000	1.06	Articles references
IOP Publishing	405,000	0.81	Articles references
RSC Publishing	360,000	0.72	Articles references
Project Euclid	122,000	0.24	Articles references
BioMed Central	118,000	0.24	Full-text articles
Crystallography Journals Online	110,000	0.22	Full-text articles
Royal Society Publishing	71,400	0.14	Full-text articles
Total	49,866,500	100.00	

the distribution of the number of documents by publisher – with PubMed (44.7 per cent), ScienceDirect (23.2 per cent) and SpringerLink (7 per cent) standing out as the organizations providing the most documents. It is interesting to note that most of the publishers made their full-text articles available only under subscription. Therefore, in the 'Journal sources' section only 6 per cent of articles (2.8 million) were open access. PubMed Central, as noted earlier, was the publishing gateway with the most open access articles (5 per cent), followed by BioMed Central (0.24 per cent) and Crystallography Journals Online (0.22 per cent).

'Preferred web sources' showed more heterogeneous content types, which also came from different and more varied sources (see Tables 3.3 and 3.4). The largest proportion (68.7 per cent) was formed by a group of patent databases accessible via LexisNexis, a database provider. These patents correspond to the patent offices of the United States (USPTO), Europe (EPO), Japan (JPO), the World Intellectual Property Organization (WIPO) and the United Kingdom (UKIPO). The second largest group was made up of institutional repositories (19.8 per cent) which housed the academic production of a wide range of organizations: the US Department of Energy (DoE) (0.85 per cent) and the Wageningen Yield (0.47 per cent) were the largest repositories in this section. The smallest sources were clustered in the Digital Archives class that represented the 16.8 per cent of 'Preferred web sources'. Thematic repositories were the third largest source type (11.5 per cent), housing academic materials related to a particular discipline. This group included NDLTD, which covers doctoral theses and other scholarly dissertations (6.1 per cent), RePEc, a specialized economics repository hosting articles and working papers (2.9 per cent), and arXiv.org, a thematic archive of e-prints covering a varied range of disciplines such as physics, mathematics and computer sciences (2.2 per cent). Finally, bibliographic databases

Table 3.3 Distribution of documents by source type in 'Preferred web sources' section

Source type	Documents	Distribution (%)
Database provider	25,500,000	68.70
Institutional repository	7,344,700	19.79
Thematic repository	4,274,200	11.51
Bibliographic database	386,000	1.04
Total	37,118,900	100.00

Table 3.4 Distribution of documents by source in 'Preferred web sources' section

Source	Source type	Documents	Distribution (%)	Document type
LexisNexis	Database provider	25,500,000	67.99	Patent records
Digital Archives	Institutional repository	6,300,000	16.80	Full-text documents
NDLTD	Thematic repository	2,300,000	6.13	Full-text theses
RePEc	Thematic repository	1,100,000	2.93	Full-text documents
arXiv.org	Thematic repository	843,000	2.25	E-print
MD Consult	Bibliographic database	365,000	0.97	Articles references
US Department of Energy	Institutional repository	319,000	0.85	Full-text documents
WaY	Institutional repository	177,600	0.47	Full-text documents
DiVA	Institutional repository	96,000	0.26	Full-text documents
University of Hong Kong	Institutional repository	92,500	0.25	Full-text documents
MIT OpenCourseWare	Institutional repository	88,000	0.23	Teaching materials
CURATOR	Institutional repository	85,500	0.23	Full-text documents
Caltech CODA	Institutional repository	50,000	0.13	Full-text documents
II Sc	Institutional repository	42,000	0.11	E-print
University of Toronto T-Space	Institutional repository	33,200	0.09	Full-text documents
Humboldt-Universität	Institutional repository	27,000	0.07	Full-text documents
NASA	Institutional repository	26,700	0.07	Reports
Organic Eprints	Thematic repository	23,400	0.06	Full-text documents
OncologySTAT	Bibliographic database	21,000	0.06	Articles references
HKUST Institutional Repository	Institutional repository	7,200	0.02	Full-text documents
CogPrints	Thematic repository	4,100	0.01	E-print
PsyDok	Thematic repository	3,700	0.01	Full-text documents
Total		37,118,900	100.00	

(1 per cent) such as MD Consult for clinical medicine (1 per cent) and OncologySTAT (0.06 per cent) completed the 'Preferred web sources' section (see Figure 3.2). In spite of the above, Scirus was one of the search engines with less coverage of open access repositories (Bhat, 2010).

In terms of the thematic coverage, 'Scirus help' (Scirus, 2013b) claimed that the web pages and digital documents were classified through a linguistic analysis of 20 scientific subject areas. The classification process was based on each web document's map of words against a dictionary or thesaurus built from a manually pre-classified corpus of scientific pages and key words extracted from specialized scientific databases. A term vector model was used to obtain a statistical likelihood of membership of each document to one class. Surprisingly, the classification scheme did not correspond to the subject area categories of Scopus (2014b), even though both services belonged to Elsevier. Moreover, the Scirus subject classification cast doubts on the subject definition and the possible overlap between subjects. For example, Social and Behavioral Sciences might contain documents from Psychology and from Sociology; similarly, Life Sciences was related to both Agricultural and Biological Sciences and Environmental Sciences. Another significant problem was that there was no Arts & Humanities classification, which meant that documents about history, literature or the arts could not be retrieved, although they were indeed included.

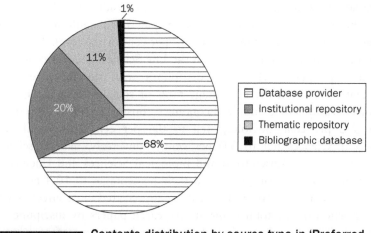

Figure 3.2 Contents distribution by source type in 'Preferred web sources' section

Because Scirus did not show the entire distribution of documents by subject classification, in July 2013 a symbolic query "a" delimited by each subject class was carried out. It is interesting to note that the sum of all the classes totalled 165 million documents. However, when a query selecting all the disciplines was launched, Scirus retrieved 556 million documents. This means that only one-third of the documents were classified, which reinforces the assumption that there was an important number of documents that were not classified either because there were no categories for them, or simply because the classification system did not manage to assign a class. This was made worse when the system assigned more than one category to a unique document, causing a significant overlap between neighbouring disciplines. Table 3.5 shows an approximated estimation of items by subject areas obtained with the previous query. The disciplines with the highest presence were the Life Sciences (14 per cent), Medicine (13.6 per cent), and Economics, Business and Management (9.2 per cent), while Languages and Linguistics (0.02 per cent) and Law (0.6 per cent) were the areas with the fewest documents. It is possible to observe the strong presence of the social science disciplines such as Economics, Business and Management, and Sociology (6.7 per cent), while areas with a prominent scientific activity such as Chemistry and Chemical Engineering (5.2 per cent) and Physics (3.8 per cent) showed a low coverage in Scirus. This particular distribution could be influenced by the sources selected and the size of those sources, although the fact that the majority of the documents were not classified means that these values must be considered with caution.

On the other hand, excluding web pages, 62 million research documents were classified in Scirus – 37 per cent of the total. Thematic distribution remained the same, with the Life Sciences (17 per cent) and Medicine (17 per cent) as the disciplines with the most research documents. However, the percentage rates of social science disciplines fell considerably. For example, Economics, Business and Management fell to 2.2 per cent, Sociology fell to 0.6 per cent and Social and Behavioral Sciences fell to 3.0 per cent. Conversely, natural science disciplines such as Agricultural and Biological Sciences and Chemistry and Chemical Engineering increased their percentages to 10.4 per cent and 9.5 per cent respectively. This will be appreciated more effectively if the proportion of the total items and research papers by disciplines is calculated. The disciplines that showed the lowest percentages were

Table 3.5 Subject area distribution of items (total and excluding web pages)

Subject area	Total	Distribution (%)	Excluding web pages	Distribution (%)	Items/articles (%)
Life Sciences	23,150,619	14.05	10,493,156	16.96	45.33
Medicine	22,464,982	13.63	10,443,999	16.88	46.49
Economics, Business and Management	15,199,834	9.22	1,390,416	2.25	9.15
Agricultural and Biological Sciences	14,454,615	8.77	6,438,093	10.40	44.54
Sociology	11,037,443	6.70	379,460	0.61	3.44
Social and Behavioural Sciences	10,330,509	6.27	1,860,935	3.01	18.01
Materials Science	9,520,093	5.78	5,615,243	9.08	58.98
Chemistry and Chemical Engineering	8,624,976	5.23	5,918,793	9.57	68.62
Engineering, Energy and Technology	7,779,126	4.72	3,980,042	6.43	51.16
Computer Science	6,786,819	4.12	1,715,193	2.77	25.27
Physics	6,331,536	3.84	3,862,023	6.24	61.00
Environmental Sciences	6,039,370	3.66	1,337,540	2.16	22.15
Pharmacology	5,831,644	3.54	3,373,178	5.45	57.84
Earth and Planetary Sciences	5,152,443	3.13	780,922	1.26	15.16
Neuroscience	3,969,830	2.41	2,336,369	3.78	58.85
Psychology	3,878,742	2.35	1,012,482	1.64	26.10
Mathematics	1,778,221	1.08	496,243	0.80	27.91
Astronomy	1,433,400	0.87	417,857	0.68	29.15
Law	1,018,114	0.62	14,290	0.02	1.40
Languages and Linguistics	34,123	0.02	9,663	0.02	28.32
All subject areas	164,816,439	100.00	61,875,897	100.00	37.54

social sciences such as Law (1.4 per cent), Sociology (3.4 per cent) and Economics, Business and Management (9.1 per cent), whereas the highest percentages were found in classical natural disciplines such as Chemistry and Chemical Engineering (68.6 per cent) and Physics (61 per cent). These differences lead me to suggest that the social sciences produce more web pages than scientific documents, while classical disciplines are almost exclusively focused on the production of research documents.

Figure 3.3 shows the distribution of documents by publication year. It is interesting to note the high degree of recency of Scirus data as 78.5 per cent of all documents corresponded to the most recent lustrum (2009–13). One possible explanation for this high proportion of recent documents could be that most of the Scirus documents were web pages which, often, are updated constantly. A study carried out on the age of web pages found that more than half of academic web pages are created or modified within a year (Ortega et al., 2009). In fact, if web pages were excluded from the search, the proportion of documents in the first lustrum would be only 18.3 per cent, and only 19.4 per cent in the second, figures comparable with other search engines.

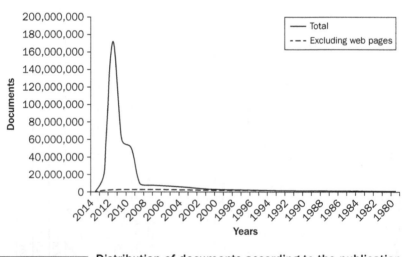

Figure 3.3 Distribution of documents according to the publication date in Scirus

Crawling and data extraction

The crawling process was detailed in a Scirus white paper (2004). It was performed on a selected list of URLs or seeds obtained in two main ways. The first procedure used an automatic URL extractor to find URLs based on a link analysis of the most popular sites in specific subject areas. This suggests that Scirus performed a random walk across the web selecting the most-linked websites. The second procedure came from the recommendation of the Elsevier publishing units and advisory members, in addition to suggestions that users brought to the search engine. Next, a crawler explored the pages hosted in those URLs or domains, avoiding extracting information from web pages not in the seed list.

However, some doubts were raised about this process. The most important was that it was not clear what content criteria were used to select the seed list. It is possible that a website is strongly 'scientific' but does not include relevant scientific information. For example, not all web pages hosted within a university web domain are scientific pages because the domain also includes information about administrative services, educational news and general information on the educational community (social events, sport activities, student blogs, etc.). Certainly, an .edu and .ac.uk domain belongs to a university website, but .org and .com domains may correspond to a wide range of institutions that can contribute scientific information in a very different way and to a very different degree. In this sense, Scirus was similar to any general-interest search engine, the only difference being that it looked for web pages previously defined as 'scientific' by a link analysis or a subjective proposal. Even so, Scirus was the most comprehensive search tool on the web that allowed launching scholarly queries on a set of pages much more pertinently than on the entire web space. As they said in their 'About us' page (Scirus, 2013a), searching for REM in Scirus will retrieve pages about sleep instead of about the rock band. So, from a scientific point of view, Scirus increased its relevance.

Nevertheless, some doubts were also raised about the database's coverage and the control of the stored web pages. For example, dynamically generated web pages were not well controlled because each one produced a new URL when it was automatically updated. The harvester bot hence stored the same page in each actualization which produced a larger list of results that pointed to the same place (see Figure 3.4). A further problem, reported by Jacsó (2008a), was that Scirus did not collapse the same record from multiple sources, generating duplicated

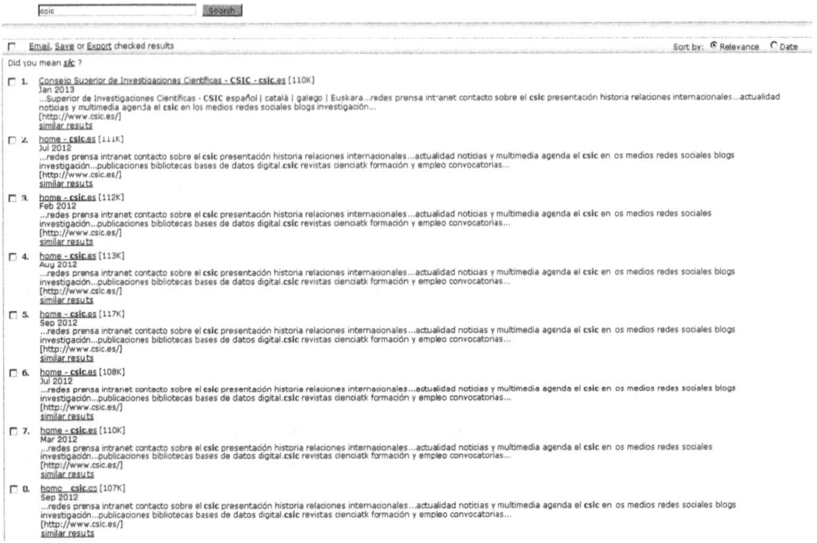

Figure 3.4

Detail of the results page of Scirus with the query "csic" (30 July 2013)

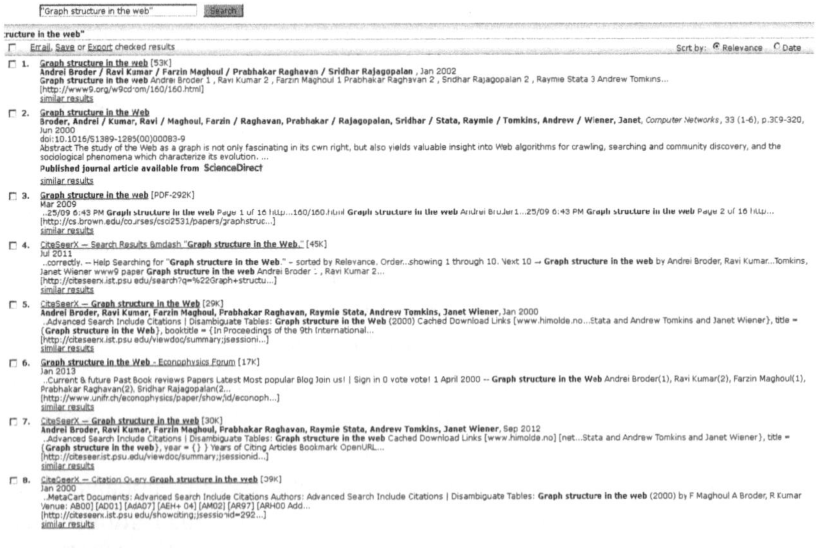

Figure 3.5

Detail of the results page of Scirus with the query "Graph structure in the web" (30 July 2013)

results. For example, an article published in ScienceDirect, deposited in an institutional repository and hung on the author's website, was retrieved three times (Figure 3.5). This resulted in a high rate of redundancy (22 per cent) and a low grade of relevancy (35 per cent) (Doldi and Bratengeyer, 2005).

Source filtering

The search system was powered by Fast Search & Transfer (FAST) – the same company that developed AlltheWeb.com and gave support to Scopus, which conferred a quality mark on the search engine. The search interface followed the classical structure of a search engine with a text box in which any search chain could be launched. The results page was divided into three differentiated parts. The first part, which occupied the top band, contained the search box, the results hits and the handling actions of the results. It is interesting to note that Scirus allowed saving up to 40 of the query results by selecting a check box. These personal results were stored, using, perhaps, cookies to identify each user. These saved results could also be downloaded to reference management software or as a plain text file.

The second part, in the left margin, corresponded to a filtering system of results based on the content sources and file types. In this way, it was possible to delimit the search by the sources used to feed Scirus, selecting documents from a concrete publisher or repository. On the other hand, the file type filter selected the results by document type. Although it might have been more interesting to filter the results by information types rather than file types, because the document typology (article, thesis, pre-print, etc.) brings more relevant information than a file type (HTML, PDF, Word, etc.). Even so, it was also possible to refine the query based on the most frequent terms, marking the most relevant words for the search. However, the principal limitation of this filtering system was that these terms could only be used to refine the query (AND) but not to extend it (OR) (Jacsó, 2008a), although this limitation was solved in the advanced search with the use of Booleans operators. 'Content sources' made it possible to select 'Journal sources' (publishers' web gateways), 'Preferred web sources' (repositories and databases) or 'Other web' (scholarly web pages).

Finally, the results section displayed the query's retrieved documents. It showed only ten results per page by default, but this could be changed to up to 100 results per page in the preferences section. These results could be sorted by relevance and date. Relevance criteria will be discussed in the ranking section.

In addition, Scirus presented one of the most complete advanced search sections, where it was possible to enhance the previous filtering system as well as to employ Booleans operators, wildcards and shortcuts. Advanced searching also made it possible to delimit the search using five criteria:

- *Dates*: Scirus allowed the user to search for documents created before 1900. Obviously these were documents created before 1900 which were transferred as scanned documents uploaded to repositories or as digitalized photographs to historical databases. It also included old issues of important journals such as *The Lancet*, *Physical Review* and *Nature*.

- *Information types*: Scirus also enabled the user to search according to a wide range of research document types, from articles to conference communications, from patents to doctoral theses. However, there were some limitations when it came to classifying certain documents within those categories. Some bibliographic records from ScienceDirect and PubMed Central were misclassified. For example: certain books were actually book chapters; conferences were really meeting and conference reports in the case of ScienceDirect, and articles published in a monographic number in PubMed Central; patents were case study articles; pre-prints in PubMed Central were simply articles, and in ScienceDirect they were post-print articles for the following months. Also, Scirus did not manage to correctly classify the Scientist homepage and it included pages that did not fit within that category.

- *File formats*: Scirus restricted the search to determinate file extensions such as HTML, PDF or DOC.

- *Content sources*: Scirus made it possible to select specific sources such as 'Journals sources' and 'Preferred web sources'. This issue is discussed in detail above (see p. 30).

- *Subject areas*: Scirus limited the search based on different research disciplines. This part is also discussed on p. 35.

Finally, the advanced search also enabled the use of several strategies for improved searching – such as Boolean operators (AND, OR and ANDNOT), quotation marks for searching an exact phrase, wildcards such as '?' to replace a single character or '*' to replace more than one. Perhaps the most interesting feature was the search for specific fields, which allowed the user to search a term by the place in which it appeared in the document. Abbreviations could be combined in the same query using Boolean operators; Table 3.6 displays the supported abbreviations.

Table 3.6   List of the abbreviations used to search specific fields

Field	Abbreviation
Author	au:
Title	ti:
Journal	jo:
Key words	ke:
URL	url:
Web domain	dom:
Author affiliation	af:

This limited search by fields could also be performed in the advanced search scroll-down box.

These abbreviations had great potential for bibliometric and webometric analyses. For instance, the combined use of affiliation fields made it possible to study collaborations at organization and country level, the author field favoured the co-author studies, and the key words could be used for co-word analyses. Webometric statistics could also be carried out with the URL and domain tips.

Ranking on links

Results could be ranked by relevance or by date. Although Scirus did not make explicit the formula that calculated the relevance, it explained that it was calculated through an algorithm based on two parameters: words and links (Scirus, 2004). Each parameter constituted 50 per cent of the final rank value. Words were defined as static values, determined by the position in which the search term occurred in the document (for example, a word in the title could be worth more than the same word in the main text) and the frequency with which that term appeared in the document. Links, on the other hand, were considered to be a dynamic score, valued according to the number of incoming links that a page received from other pages. The final rank was calculated from the weighted sum of both values. Scirus also advised that it did not operate with meta tags because, it argued, users could modify the rank artificially. However, while this is valid for web pages that are connected by hyperlinks, other materials such as research papers, dissertations or conference proceedings are not always associated by links, so the relevance, in my opinion, could be distorted without assessment criteria such as citations.

A missed opportunity

This examination of Scirus's capabilities allows us to draw some conclusions as to its advantages and disadvantages. Scirus was presented as a comprehensive search engine that acted as a gateway to a wide range of scientific documents from a heterogeneous variety of sources, where the web content occupied the greatest proportion. This made Scirus the only academic search engine that indexed web pages from scholarly sites. This bold decision made it possible for a user to retrieve a large number of scientific documents, but there was also the danger that many of these retrieved documents could be very broad in content, or that they could be merely navigational pages with content of low relevance (Mayr and Walter, 2007). These web pages needed to undergo a meticulous filtering process that would extract only relevant pages that would contribute valuable scientific information. Perhaps, then, the most important aspects of this academic tool were the great variety of sources that fed the non-web section and the potential to select desired databases exactly when needed. The advanced search function of Scirus was the most complete of the academic search engines analysed, making it possible to obtain a general picture of its contents (Medeiros, 2002).

As stated above, however, certain technical limitations meant that Elsevier's product did not accomplish its aims as effectively as it should have done. The principal limitation revolved around its classification system. Two-thirds of the total number of documents were not assigned to any class category which meant that there was no way of knowing the search engine's actual coverage from a subject point of view. This problem extended to the 'Information type' classification where some documents were erroneously assigned to certain information types, especially those from ScienceDirect and PubMed Central. This cast doubts on the effectiveness of its classification system. The classification scheme could also have been reinforced by adding important categories such as 'Arts & Humanities' and by adapting it to fit earlier classification systems such as the Scopus Subject Areas (another Elsevier service). This would have produced a more realistic distribution of the documents included in the Scirus search engine.

Other minor technical failures were observed in Scirus's data harvesting. It was not clear that the seeds selection process was based on a mixed procedure of link analysis and subjective inclusion. This process should have been more transparent, detailing how the link analysis worked and how and why suggestions made by Elsevier's staff were accepted. This point is relevant when it comes to the issue of feeding the search engine with pertinent and high-quality content. Another problem that should have been reviewed was the control and cleaning of the crawled web pages because, as was observed in Figures 3.3 and 3.4, Scirus indexed duplicated records which produced noise and inefficiency in the search results.

In summary, Scirus was a suitable and recommendable tool for searching scientific information because it was the only academic search engine which directly crawled scholarly web pages and complemented the results with the most comprehensive scientific sources available on the web. The correction of the aforementioned technical limitations could have increased the potential and performance of this service for the scientific community, and, maybe, could have helped prevent its closure.

The closure of Scirus was a hard loss for the academic search engine market. Its deep coverage of academic web pages, its transparent collection of scientific sources and a search interface based on filters were original contributions that could have served in the design of new solutions or improved current solutions. Products such as Q-Sensei Scholar or WorldWideScience.org with their filtering search interfaces, or Google Scholar with its mixture of web and publisher sources, have taken Scirus as their reference. In my opinion, Elsevier closed Scirus prematurely, because this engine still had good functionality and interesting features to share with the scientific community.

4

AMiner: science networking
as an information source

Abstract: Tsinghua University in China first introduced the concept of the personal profile, an element that revolves around the entire structure of its search engine. In addition, it also presented several visualization instruments and elaborated information that enrich the assessment of authors and venues. However, the service also contains several anomalies and inconsistencies, such as a deficient search mechanism, a lack of source transparency, and a chaotic and unsuccessful design. These rather serious problems undermine the user's trust in this tool as a reliable source not only for research evaluation but also for academic information retrieval.

Key words: AMiner, Tsinghua University, PatentMiner, co-authorship, Author-Conference-Topic.

AMiner (formerly ArnetMiner) (*http://www.arnetminer.org*) was created in 2006 by Jie Tang's team in the Department of Computer Science and Technology at Tsinghua University in China. AMiner is the result of a research project on scientific social networks, the main objective of which was to describe the networking patterns in science through co-authored papers. From that idea, AMiner introduced a new perspective focused on the author as the central element in an academic search engine. In this sense, the complete service revolves around personal profiles, attempting to be a search tool more focused on the retrieval of profiles than documents. Thus, AMiner can be considered to be the first web searching service to introduce the profiling concept, displaying an author's entire curricula which can be browsed through collaboration links between authors. In this way, AMiner displaces the document as the centre of scientific searching, and focuses its attention on personal profiles as the basic unit of scientific activity.

A networked engine

AMiner is an academic search engine that was born as a research project addressed to build and analyse scientific social networks. With that purpose in mind, AMiner relies on personal profiles as the foundation for the structure of the entire search platform. Five stages were implemented in the construction of the search engine system (Tang et al., 2007; Tang et al., 2008).

- In the first stage, AMiner proceeds to the data extraction of two differentiated entities: authors and documents. Unlike other search engines, AMiner does not directly extract authors from documents, but instead crawls the web looking for personal homepages, identifying and collecting names. Tang et al. (2008), in their seminal paper on AMiner's methodology, claim that the author's name is used to identify the homepage of each researcher. They use Google API to automatically query to the search engine and then identify the homepage from the results. Each author is characterized according to a FOAF scheme, in which the principal attributes that identify a researcher – such as institutional affiliation, address, research interests and a brief academic curriculum – are included. However, they do not clarify from where they obtain that list of names – whether the names are extracted from a web crawling or from other bibliographic sources. Therefore, it is possible to imagine that the engine uses other sources to obtain the names. In a conference paper, Zhang et al. (2008) explain that they utilize Libra (Microsoft Academic Search since 2009) and Rexa systems to extract the experts' name list. Once the authors list is defined, the system extracts the authors' bibliographic information from publicly accessible web sources such as search engines (CiteSeer[x]), digital libraries (Association for Computing Machinery [ACM]), web bibliographic databases (Digital Bibliography & Library Project [DBLP]), among others.

- The second stage is the integration and assignation of publications to the authors. This process implies a certain ambiguity because different authors may share similar names or an author may publish under different name variants. AMiner uses a probabilistic framework to solve the name ambiguity problem in the integration stage. This framework is based on Hidden Markov Random Fields (HMRF), a probabilistic model based on a Markov process but with unobserved states, and is used to assign each author to their papers. Five variables are considered in order to calculate the probability of belonging of a document to the same name: venue (papers published in the same journal or conference), co-author (similar co-authors on a paper), citation (paper cited by other papers), constraint (feedback suggested by users) and extension of co-authorship (similar co-authors on other papers). In this way, AMiner disambiguates authors' names, finding similar patterns in papers with similar publishing properties. Finally, the integrated data is stored on a researcher network knowledge base (RNKB).

- The third stage – storage and access – hosts and indexes the extracted/integrated data in the RNKB. Specifically, MySQL is employed for storage, with an inverted file for indexing.

- Next – in the modelling phase – documents are categorized using a generative probabilistic pattern. This is based on a model called Author-Conference-Topic (ACT). According to this model, the words used to describe each document are related to the venue in which the paper is published, the collaborating co-authors and the topics discussed in the papers. This model estimates a topic probability for each type of item: author, venue and paper.

- Finally, the search services constitute the different access points used by the system to retrieve the information on authors and papers.

A chaotic design

AMiner is structured in seven differentiated sections which gather the principal search services and functionalities that the search engine offers. In the main page, these sections are presented in a top menu. However, in the main search box you can see another seven sections in a different menu. This is rather confusing because some sections with different names point to the same site, while other sections do not correspond to the second menu (Figure 4.1).

A new element incorporated quite recently is a picture on the homepage that graphically illustrates the evolution of a discipline, for example Artificial Intelligence (AI) (Figure 4.1). A link below points to another similar map on 'AMiner's History', but both do not work. These images show the longitudinal evolution of a discipline, with new branches emerging all the time. However, the images are not inserted into any section and no explanation exists about their meaning. Thus, it is not possible to know if these elements have some searchable

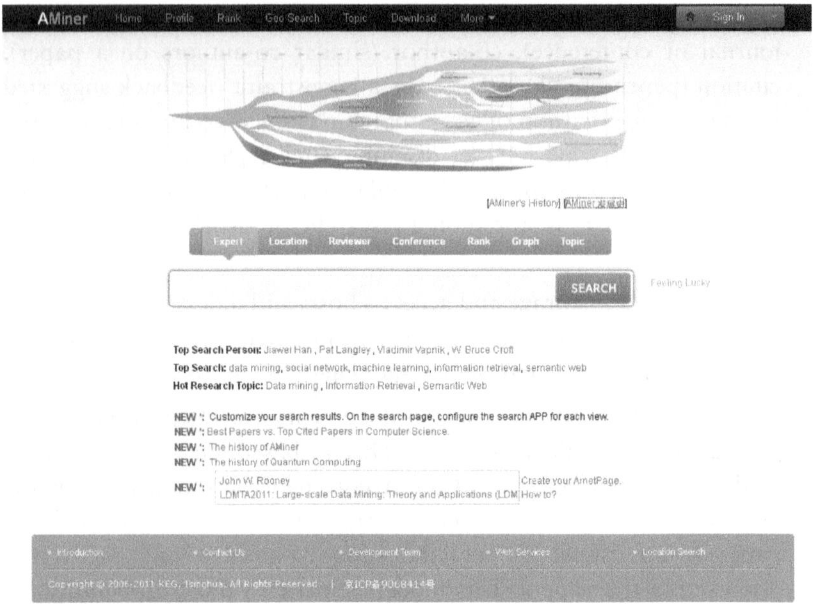

Figure 4.1 Homepage of AMiner (21 February 2014)

functionality or if they are simply graphical representations of research disciplines.

However, to return to the organizing structure of AMiner, seven sections are labelled in the top menu:

- 'Home': this page shows a registration box where a user can sign in. This allows her/him to suggest changes and modifications to the records and the personal profiles. Once registered, users can link to a profile to edit its curriculum and biography. Unlike other profiling services, these modifications can be applied to any profile, which could result in the intentional loss of information, or the hacking of researchers' personal biographies, as well as the uploading of non-reviewed papers (see Figure 4.2). However, it is surprising that this functionality does not allow the user to suggest the removal, adaptation or merging of duplicate and erroneous profiles, in addition to the correction of the list of publications. This should be the main purpose of this section – to facilitate the personal maintenance of each personal profile.

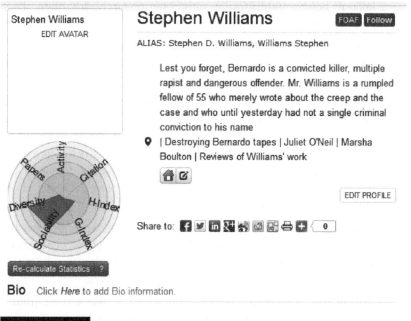

Stephen Williams
EDIT AVATAR

Stephen Williams   FOAF Follow

ALIAS: Stephen D. Williams, Williams Stephen

Lest you forget, Bernardo is a convicted killer, multiple rapist and dangerous offender. Mr. Williams is a rumpled fellow of 55 who merely wrote about the creep and the case and who until yesterday had not a single criminal conviction to his name

📍 | Destroying Bernardo tapes | Juliet O'Neil | Marsha Boulton | Reviews of Williams' work

EDIT PROFILE

Share to: 　　　　　　　　　　 0

Re-calculate Statistics   ?

Bio   Click *Here* to add Bio information.

Figure 4.2   An example of a spoiled profile

- 'Profile': this is the principal section of the search engine and presents the personal profiles bound to the user's personal account (see Figure 4.5 on p. 62). If the user is not logged in, it shows the main search page where authors can be sought by free text. This will be examined in detail in the Profiles section.

- 'Rank': this function displays a ranking of personal profiles according to several bibliometric indicators, some of them defined *ad hoc* by AMiner and obtained from the structural analysis of collaboration patterns. This ranking shows 1,253,433 profiles, organized by the following indicators: h-index, g-index, #paper, citation, diversity, sociability, new star, rising star and activity. These academic statistics are sketched out in detail in a draft document of the group, although some indicators used are not described, such as the g-index or rising star (Wang et al., 2014). Only indicators created by AMiner are commented upon below:

  - 'Diversity': this is a measure of the multidisciplinarity of an author according to the ACT model defined by AMiner. Thus, the indicator rises if a researcher works across different topics, and falls if he/she publishes in only one research discipline. It is measured in a logarithmic scale.

- 'Sociability': this counts the number of different co-authors that a researcher has – understood as an index of social interaction. It is also measured in a logarithmic scale.

- 'Activity': this indicator values the complete production of an author, focusing on the most recently published papers. This rewards those authors with the most recent publishing activity, as opposed to authors with an intermittent or historical scientific performance. However, this advantage is only considered for the previous five years, then the indicator favours consolidated authors with an extensive career.

- 'New star': this is the opposite of the 'Activity' measure because the 'New star' index considers only the previous five years' production, and is the indicator where younger authors, with a good activity rate, are more highly valued than older researchers.

- 'Rising star': this indicator is not described in Wang et al. (ibid.), although they do define 'uptrend' as the 'rising degree of a researcher', and in older versions this was called the 'Uptrend' indicator, instead of 'Rising star'. This value varies according to each research topic and tries to predict the future rating of an author in each topic from the date of their papers and the impact factor of the journals in which he/she publishes. It is interesting to see that a variant of the impact factor (Journal Impact Factor is a proprietary algorithm owned by Thomson Reuters) is used to value journals and conferences; however, it does not publish any journal ranking and nor does it show the impact value for each journal as an indicator on each journal/conference page. This new definition includes the length of a paper as a criterion to determine the impact of a journal. Despite the relationship between length and citations which has been described (Falagas et al., 2013), there could exist different publishing patterns between disciplines that affect the article length.

- 'Geo Search': this section makes it possible to carry out a search in which the results are displayed in a geographical world map from Google Maps. This interface allows the user to geographically locate authors who work in a discipline and to observe the spatial distribution of research topics across countries and regions. It is difficult to know exactly how this application works because the term search retrieves inconsistent results. I suspect that it works like a general search, performed on the documents instead of the profiles. This means that if you are looking for German researchers, the system retrieves authors from anywhere which uses the term German in its publications. One other problem is the geo-location of each author in the map, because there are author profiles situated in a different place to that given in the contact address. This could occur with authors who have worked in different places – perhaps the system takes the first or the most frequent place of work from the publications' correspondence. It is not known what proportion of allocations are incorrect, but any query would probably return some examples of this. Finally, this resource is limited to the indexation of only the first 1000 authors by h-index, giving a limited view of a research topic.

- 'Topic': AMiner classifies each research paper according to the aforementioned ACT model. Thus, each document is characterized by the 200 research topics that are defined by the search engine a priori. These topics are principally related to computer science and other disciplines such as physics, mathematics, bioinformatics, information sciences, etc. The topics are composed of two labels that are present in several topics, meaning that the topics show enough overlap between them. For example, the 'Wireless network' label appears in six topics, 'Knowledge management' appears in four, and 'Software engineering' also appears in four. There are also confusing terms that lack any meaning by themselves, or for which their relationships are unclear and incoherent. For instance, in 'Dynamic networks/Extended abstract', I do not understand the meaning of 'Extended abstract' as a research topic nor do I understand its relationship with 'Dynamic networks'. Further, there are absurd connections such as 'Low power electronics design/New York' and 'Digital government/Case study'. The topic browser page lists the complete ranking of these topics, and within each one it shows the six most representative authors by number of papers assigned to each category, as well as including the four most important journals related to each topic.

A more detailed view of each topic can be obtained by clicking the title. This page (Figure 4.3) specifies the terms that define each topic and the authors and venues associated with it. Thus, each topic page displays the 'hot words' that characterize each topic. These words are taken from the title of the publications and their sources (journals and conferences) following the ACT model. Beside each hot word – in parentheses – is the probability of each word belonging to that topic. Clearly, however, there is no cleaning nor blocking process that

Figure 4.3   Topic page from AMiner (21 February 2014)

removes synonyms, meaningless words and terms with the same stem. For example, the most relevant words in Topic 1 are 'systems' and 'system' which are the same word, followed by 'based' and 'approach', both words with a very broad, general meaning. These words have little distinguishing power and they complicate the assignation of a paper to one or other topic. This allocation process is also carried out on the basis of the likelihood of a journal belonging to one topic. The most relevant journals and conferences are ranked on the right-hand side of the page. Scrolling down the middle of the page, you will notice a trend chart in which the evolution of the most significant topic words is plotted. It would appear that there is a threshold for the inclusion of these words because some figures do not display all the terms. Moving again to the right-hand side of the page, the most relevant articles in each category are listed. Further down the middle of the page, the 'active inventors [*sic*]' within a topic are listed, as are the popular phrases from the titles of papers, and as is a new chart showing the evolution of the number of papers in the topic through the years.

In summary, this page aims to show the words, venues, titles and authors linked to a research topic as a means of grouping them under a subject matter classification and improving the information retrieval. The charts add interesting data that describe the evolution of terms and topics, which could be useful for the analysis of scientific dynamics over time. Nevertheless, and in terms of its use as a search engine, this section presents irrelevant information such as hot words and popular phrases that do not contribute to the searchability of documents and authors, and the information presented can be confusing. Moreover, the inclusion of important information such as the number of documents or authors within each category or connections between topics would improve the use and enrich the value of this section.

- 'Download': this section makes it possible to discharge raw data obtained from different crawls performed by AMiner's research group. These data are subsets from the AMiner initiative and they are freely available for help with new research projects. These data sets are explained in detail and the usual formats are plain text and XML. Data collections represent distinct projects carried out around AMiner and can include data on profiles and co-author networks to document descriptions. This section also includes data sets not related to AMiner such as Twitter followers, mobile contacts and emails' senders networks.

- ‘More’: this last section contains several applications connected with AMiner and useful for scientific social networking:

  - ‘Introduction’: this ‘about us’ page briefly describes the main functionalities of AMiner.

  - ‘Ranks’: this application is the same as that mentioned in the section on Rank above (see p. 51). (see p. 51)

  - ‘ArnetPage’: this is a web hosting service developed by AMiner allowing researchers to create and maintain personal web pages. Currently, it contains close to 500 personal websites, although many are simply outlines of the final versions of future websites or are used by the AMiner team to create help pages.

  - ‘Graph Search’: this is an application that helps plot graphs of collaboration relationships between profiles included in the database. It presents each network’s profile with that of their co-authors and facilitates the addition of new ego networks that are again connected between them, showing a complete panorama of the collaboration relationships of a group of researchers. However, this tool does not work well; it is very slow and the graph is not displayed in its entirety, in spite of having been tried with the most popular web browsers (Mozilla Firefox, Internet Explorer and Google Chrome). It also has problems identifying authors included in the database, and it is not able to display the networks of those authors.

  - ‘Collaborator Recommendation’: this is a tool similar to CollabSeer by CiteSeer[x] but it is more detailed because it retrieves similar profiles according to their publication interests, as a means of looking up partners with common interests. It is structured in three parts: a tree map with the target domain and associated research topics; a recommended list of authors; and a ranking of the most cited papers in the target domain. The system defines a default target domain for the selected profile, although this can be changed within ‘Target domain and your background’. The results page first shows a tree map with the topics that match the target domain, but a closer inspection highlights some concerns. For example, if selecting ‘World Wide Web’ as a domain, the most relevant topics retrieved are ‘Mobile robots/Hybrid control’, ‘Wireless networks/ Cellular systems’ or ‘Wavelet image coding/Video compression’, all of which are more closely related to ‘Internet’ or ‘Communications network’ than with the web. This is an important failure because the system selects the advising authors from these topics. In my case, for example, I was advised to collaborate with engineers in robotics or communications networks, rather than with information scientists or web search researchers. The tree map includes the most relevant authors by topic in proportional rectangles to the h-index, although this is merely a visual perception. This map is rather confusing because it does not display any information about the configuration of the boxes, and relevant authors in the recommendation list are omitted from the graph. As with the CollabSeer service, these automatic services do not capture the complex mechanisms that generate a collaboration process and the suggestions do not match the users' needs. Not least because the search for partners changes over time and is influenced by important external variables such as funding, geographical distance, disciplines, etc. (Katz and Martin, 1997).

- 'Reviewer Recommendation': as above, this service is supposed to recommend referees for an article. It is necessary to be logged in to use it, although it does not work in many cases.

Based on bibliographic databases

AMiner's 'Introduction' page claims that the search engine includes more than 3.2 million papers, 700,000 research profiles and 6000 conference communications (AMiner, 2010). AMiner assigns a number to each profile; on looking at the last profile in the database, 1,636,950 possible profiles were detected in February 2013. However, on looking for the last profile in the papers' ranking section, 1,253,433 profiles were found. I suspect that the difference could be due to undocumented profiles, disused profiles or profiles that have been removed.

In any case, the above leads us to suppose that the number of profiles has almost doubled in three years, which is a significant growth. Unfortunately, however, it is impossible to obtain more information on the distribution of these authors and papers, and on the sources that feed these data. Not least because the engine lacks a simple advanced search, and because the searchable units are not indexed in an independent form. The only section that can contribute some information on coverage is the 'Conference/Journal' section, which lists the titles and the number of papers indexed by AMiner. Upon harvesting this section, the total number of papers (including conference papers) is given as 2,459,904, 76.8 per cent of the total number proclaimed by the engine (ibid.). This difference could be due to an inability to assign a venue to the remaining papers, which therefore are not displayed in this section, or it could be that those non-accessible items simply do not exist. My figure coincides with that of DBLP, which gathered 2.5 million items in February 2014. The other sections of the engine do not reveal the total number of documents grouped by topics or profiles.

AMiner is a search service built on multiple open access sources that are available on the web. In this way, AMiner provides a cocktail of data from multiple sources that are assembled to form a search engine of scientific documents and profiles. But, unlike Scirus or Google Scholar which act as hubs that distribute access to open sources, AMiner appropriates data without any reference to its sources, giving the impression that AMiner itself has crawled and harvested all the information that it displays. Examining the literature published by Tang's group, the search engine is the owner of only the list of authors, which was obtained by crawling personal web pages and extracting the names of the researchers, and the list of topics obtained through the ACT model. The rest of the information has been taken from digital libraries and thematic repositories. In Tang et al. (2008), the authors explain that they take the documents from several web databases and digital libraries such as DBLP, ACM Digital Library, Citeseer and others, but they do not say anything about what proportion of the documents is extracted from these sites, nor do they identify the original source of the documents. This makes it impossible to analyse the coverage of the engine and, as was said earlier, this introduces an ethical problem. The same is true of the citations used to calculate indicators and rank profiles, they are taken directly from Google Scholar without any explanation. Conference and journal titles are also obtained mostly from DBLP and CiteSeer[x], reproducing the same mistakes from the original sources.

Based on the thematic distribution of content, essentially AMiner includes only papers and authors from computer science and related disciplines because so many of their sources are specialized resources in that field – such as DBLP or the ACM Digital Library. This is reflected in the 'Topic Browse' section, all of which address computing issues.

Searching only in documents

As was highlighted in the structure section above (p. 49), the search menu is rather confusing and is similar to the general menu. In fact,

'Location' corresponds to 'Geo Search', 'Reviewer' corresponds to 'Reviewer Recommendation' and 'Graph' corresponds to 'Graph Search'. The remaining search sections do not give access to a search form – for example, 'Conference' points to a list of publication venues, and 'Topic' to the pre-defined list of topics. Only 'Expert', 'Location' and 'Graph' point to a search interface – 'Location' and 'Graph' having already been analysed in the structure section above (p. 52).

In the 'Expert' search, the results page is structured around three default sections that can be customized if the user is registered: 'Experts', 'Conference/Journals' and 'Publications' (see Figure 4.4). Here it would appear that the search unit is not the document but the author's profile, because when a query is launched in the 'Expert' search it only retrieves profiles according to the researcher's name; the other elements used to retrieve profiles are the title and abstract of the indexed papers linked to each profile. In actual fact, AMiner is simply a standard search engine that retrieves only documents, even though it also includes the author's name as a retrievable element. It is surprising that an 'Expert' search looks for document-related elements rather than elements based on the profile description itself. Thus, paradoxically, if you are looking for

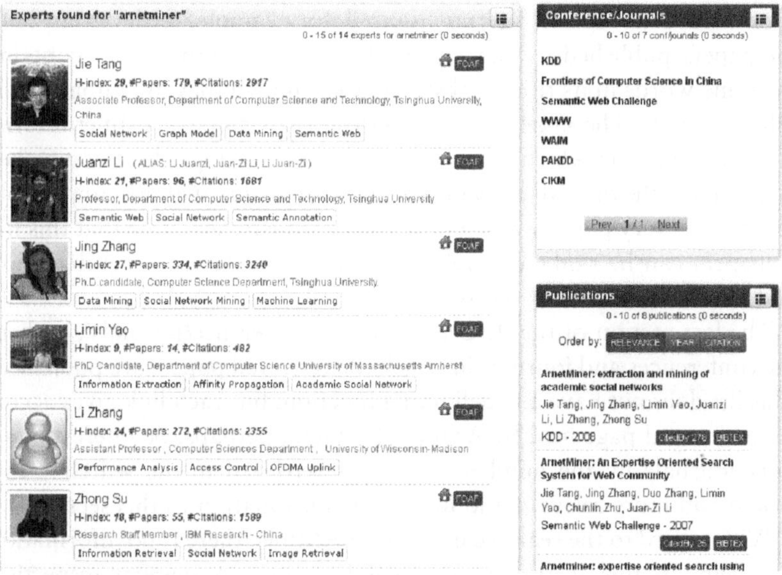

Figure 4.4 Expert results page within AMiner (24 February 2014)

members of SCImago (an important Spanish research group with expertise in bibliometrics, and responsible for the SCImago Journal Rank), some relevant authors are not retrieved because the word 'SCImago' does not appear in their papers, even though it is clearly present in their affiliations. Equally, authors that simply discuss their products are retrieved as SCImago experts because they mention the word 'SCImago' in their title. Clearly, this is not an expert search, because it should allow the user to retrieve profiles according to affiliation, country, research interest, biography, and so on, and to combine these elements in the search. As it is, the results contain much noise and imprecise information, making it barely useful as an interface with which to locate researchers in AMiner. The results ranking is also difficult to assess, because the search is performed on the papers not on the profiles. I presume that the results are arranged on the frequency of appearance of these authors in the retrieved papers, following a vector space model (Tang et al., 2007) that calculates the degree of similarity between query and documents.

Still within the 'Expert' search, the 'Publications' element lists articles that match the terms of a query. The papers are returned through four elements: title, abstract, venue and author name. However, the three first elements are not independently indexed, but indexed instead as the full text of the paper, so it is not possible to delimit a search. Thus, a search for articles published in a certain journal, for example, retrieves not only the papers published in that journal but every document that contains the same words in its title or abstract, even though they are published in other journals. The same is true with the author name – AMiner returns every document in which the author name appears, regardless of whether it appears in the title, abstract or venue, which makes it almost impossible to retrieve every paper written by a specific researcher. Note that this list of papers can be ranked by relevance to the query, year of publication and number of citations received.

The last section of the 'Expert' search, 'Conference/Journals', gathers the conferences and journals in which the retrieved papers are published. This list does not have any delimiting function, but each link gives access to the journal page held by AMiner. It would, perhaps, be interesting to rank journals by the number of articles retrieved in the search – this would add more relevant and interesting information to this section.

With regard to the search capacities of AMiner, there is no information nor help on this feature of the search engine. A manual inspection indicates that most of the elemental search features are not present in this service. For example, Boolean operators are not supported because the engine does not distinguish between OR and AND operators – a search within quotation marks returns the same matches as a search without quotations marks. The engine is also sensitive to written accents and other special characters, which prevents the retrieval of the same name written in different ways – for example, José and Jose or Müller and Mueller. There are no tips that might make it possible to delimit a search and improve the quality of a query. This is exemplified by the absence of an advance search form to filter results and limit a search to a specific criterion (Freund et al., 2012).

Essentially, AMiner generates a poor search experience because the content indexation rests on the papers, the centre of the search mechanism. Yet, with a service subtitled 'Academic Researcher Social Network Search', it really should focus its search architecture on profiles and social networking environments. Thus, AMiner needs to develop a true retrieval system that enables the utilization of these data in a more efficient way.

Exhaustive author profiles

AMiner arose out of a research project on scientific social networking and as a result aims to be a search engine focused on the personal profiles of researchers and their co-authorship connections. For this reason, AMiner is the search service which presents the most information on a researcher, forming almost a complete curriculum of each scientist. As was said in the section on functioning (p. 48), each name is taken from a web crawl of personal pages, with publication information and co-author relationships taken from DBLP, ACM Digital Library and CiteSeer[x]. Hence, the only information shown in a profile is the list of publications and the research topics defined by AMiner; the remaining data have to be edited by each user. However, within this automatic process it is usual for the system to detect multiple profiles for the same author, due to the different ways in which a researcher's name can appear in a publication.

Profiles are headed by the author's name and the various aliases used in their publications (Figure 4.5). Below this, each user can edit his/her full postal address, contact telephone number and email, and upload a recent photograph. In the top right-hand side of the page, structural information is presented on the co-author relationships of each profile. This information can be visualized in three different ways: as an ego

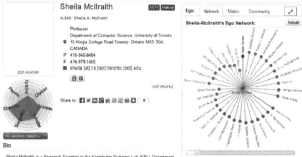

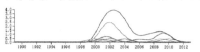

Figure 4.5   A full personal profile within AMiner (24 February 2014)

network, as a matrix and as an energized network depicting the full connections between partners but without the ego. Both ego and community would be expressed as a real ego network in which the researcher is included in a completely connected network, enriching the collaboration information of each author within his/her scientific context. Regardless, the inclusion of this information is an original feature that allows the user to study the research environment of an author. We must not forget that AMiner was born as a scientific social network analysis project, so the presentation of this data is a key element in the search service. Moreover, the service should aim to expand this relevant information and design new applications that would make it possible to browse partner profiles through these graphs, improving the search experience further.

On the left side of the page, AMiner computes several bibliometric indicators that were explained in the structure section above (p. 51). It is interesting to note that they are displayed using a pop-up window and a radial graph to highlight the scientific performance of each author in the easiest and most intuitive way.

Scrolling down the profile, the next element is the 'Bio', where each author can write about his/her life, employment and research experiences. Below this, users can register their academic qualifications in an 'Education' section. To the right of this, and under the co-author information, the page displays each author's areas of expertise and the principal venues in which he/she publishes. The expertise is drawn from the a priori research topics used to classify each research paper, while the publication sources are based on AMiner's journal list. These publication sources are sorted based on the total number of articles in brackets.

Further down the page, the 'Research Interest' is shown on the left-hand side, while the right-hand side describes the 'Key Terms'. The former gathers the labels written by the user him-/herself, while the latter compiles key words – defined by AMiner – that describe the content of the papers. It would appear that these key words are taken from the article title in a raw form, without normalizing and removing similar tags. These are accompanied by a 'Publication Statistics Line Chart' which shows the evolution of these key words over time. This is an interactive graph that allows the user to select particular key words and observe their trends, highlighting how an author's research activity evolves and changes from one scientific field to another. However, the vertical axis shows a confusing scale which seems to be the proportion of papers that contain each key word multiplied by the total number of published items – although this is conjecture on my part.

Finally, at the bottom of the page, 'Publications' lists the titles of publications that AMiner has gathered from this profile, grouping them by year or by topics. In this view, each article contains the title, authors, venue and year.

Conferences/journals

This section includes all the journals covered by AMiner. It is important to remember that these are taken from several sources mainly DBLP, ACM Digital Library and Citeseer[x] and can be ranked alphabetically or by number of papers indexed in the search engine.

Table 4.1 displays the distribution of the most important titles by number of papers. An initial observation of the listed sources is that there is no standardization in terms of the presentation of conference and journal titles. Some conference titles are presented as acronyms, and a non-expert user in these fields might not understand what *ICRA* or *ICC* mean. In addition, some journal titles are displayed in abbreviated form, such as *Commun. ACM* or *Theor. Comput. Sci.*, which impedes their retrieval. It should also be noted that CoRR (Computing Research Repository) is part of the arXiv.org repository, so it seems that AMiner gathers documents from thematic repositories as well.

Table 4.1 The most important titles in AMiner by number of papers

Conference/journal title	Papers	Distribution (%)
CoRR	59,867	2.4
IEICE Transactions	14,830	0.6
ICRA	14,134	0.6
IEEE Transactions on Information Theory	12,430	0.5
ICC	12,410	0.5
GLOBECOM	11,388	0.5
Discrete Mathematics	11,305	0.4
IROS	10,939	0.4
Applied Mathematics and Computation	10,466	0.4
Communications of the ACM	10,362	0.4
All conferences/journals	2,459,904	100.00

An effect of this lack of standardization is observed in the distribution of journals' and conferences' titles. Thus it can be observed that 16.6 per cent of the titles – AMiner lists 9630 titles – contain less than ten papers, and 9.7 per cent contain only one paper. Titles with only one paper are clearly unpublished items from repositories or extracted from CiteSeer[x], the others could be chapters of books, small symposia or workshops with low circulation. But the lack of standardization is also found in several titles that correspond to different calls from the same conference and others that bring together all the papers published in a conference. For example, the ACM Multimedia Conference shows three entries: ACM Multimedia (3372 papers), ACM Multimedia (1) (65 papers) and ACM Multimedia (2) (67 papers). Clearly, these three titles correspond to the same conference – in 1999 this conference published its proceeding in two volumes – but here these two volumes are presented as different titles when in fact they correspond to the same. This pattern is also observed in conferences which suffer changes to their name over time, with the result that AMiner presents them as different titles. These errors come from DBLP, from where these data originate, but this does not release AMiner from a responsibility to repair these failures and adopt a serious data cleaning process.

Selecting a title from the 'Conference/Journal' list, AMiner displays an individual report of each venue (Figure 4.6). This page presents statistical information that highlights the different bibliometric impact trends of each journal and the authors who publish in these sources. The first element is a search form that delimits the list of articles by year(s) and by number of results. This tool makes it possible to review the performance of a journal in a specific period and delimit the most cited papers in each journal. A manual inspection shows that there is no data for 2013 and very little for 2012.

Two charts are then displayed, based on what has been entered in the search box. On the left, a pie chart shows the distribution of the nationality of the authors that publish in the journal and, on the right, a bar chart describes the distribution of the 100 most-cited works by year. These interesting graphics provide the user with a picture of the performance of each venue over time. However, the relevance of the pie chart is limited because the authors' nationality distribution is only significant if it shows an unbalanced bias to a certain country, evidencing a local journal. Perhaps the most important issue concerns the question of how the nationality of an author is determined, given that this is an editable element in the profile section.

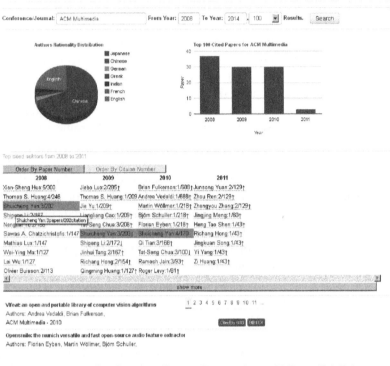

Figure 4.6 'Conference/Journal' page from AMiner (24 February 2014)

It is possible that the pie chart contains only those authors who have previously formatted the profile with that datum. But an examination of a journal as well-known as the *Journal of Informetrics* in 2008 generates a strange distribution because the nationality of the listed authors does not correspond to the pie chart at all. Looking closely at other examples, it would be reasonable to suggest that AMiner classifies only nine or ten nationalities, because these nationalities recur in all the pie charts, and the rest are simply erased. Therefore when Dutch, Spanish or Italian researchers predominate in a distribution, they are not represented in the pie chart.

Further down the displayed page, the section ranks authors either by number of papers or by number of citations in each year, which allows the user to see the most prominent authors in each venue and in a particular period. Finally, the page highlights all the journal's indexed papers, sorted by citations.

PatentMiner

In addition to AMiner, the Department of Computer Science and Technology at Tsinghua University houses a search engine specialized in patents. Because this is a service independent of AMiner I will only give a brief summary of its functions here. PatentMiner (Tang et al., 2012) is fed from the world's five most important patent offices: the USPTO in the United States, the JPO in Japan, Germany's DPMA, the IPO in the United Kingdom and Canada's CIPO. Like AMiner, its search architecture is poor and it only indexes the article title, résumé, authors and company names, but there is no list nor ranking of inventors or companies that would provide any information on performance. To obtain information on any inventor, company or subject class, it is necessary to launch a generic search in one of the two search boxes on the main page.

The results page shows all the records in which the words used in the title, résumé, inventors and company name appear, making it impossible to delimit the search to obtain an exact match, providing noisy and irrelevant results (Figure 4.7). As with AMiner, the upper part of the page shows a

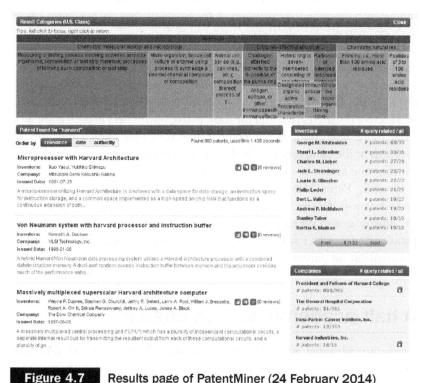

Figure 4.7   Results page of PatentMiner (24 February 2014)

tree map which classifies the retrieved patents according to the USPTO patent classification. This scheme can be use to thematically expand or refine the query. However, often the query terms do not fit the classifications and strange tree maps can be returned. For example, when searching for 'data mining' the tree map displays mining and earth science technologies.

Immediately beneath the tree map, the recorded patents – showing the title, inventors, company name, date and abstract – are returned. These results can be ordered by relevance, date and authority. Relevance is defined using a vector space model that calculates the degree of similarity of a query with the document, while the authority criterion orders the patents by the most active inventors in the field. This links up with the two sections on the right-hand side, where PatentMiner displays a ranking of inventors and companies that match up with the query. These sections sort inventors and companies by the relationship between the number of retrieved patents and the total number of patents in the system, as a measure of adaptation between the query and the system.

Clicking on each patent record, a page displays in detail the claims and currency of the patent, but there is neither a description nor a classification of the invention. The inventor page contains two trend maps by year and topic which describe the evolution of the inventor, and the complete list of authored patents. Finally, the company page does display a more complete profile of each company – with identification data such as number of employees and the date on which the company was founded. Furthermore, this page presents several trend graphs of topics and inventors that describe the technological evolution of the organization over time, detecting the most active research areas and the most active researchers in each company. Even more interesting is the comparative tool that allows the user to benchmark the company's technological performance against competitors, showing the inventive context in which an organization is located.

Overall, PatentMiner is more advanced than AMiner because it provides more detailed information about the technological performance of companies and inventors. Nevertheless, it does not solve the searching problems of its sister system and it fails to retrieve precise and exhaustive information on patents.

A half-academic search engine

Unlike a traditional academic search engine, AMiner is a web directory of researchers because the principal retrievable element is authors rather than documents. As mentioned previously, AMiner revolves around the author profiles, providing a complete and editable curriculum for each author. Perhaps the most interesting feature of AMiner is the focus on co-authors and their relationships, making this service an original tool for scientific collaboration analysis. This is accompanied by the option to edit profiles, which encourages the participation of users and increases the accuracy of the information provided for each author. In this sense, AMiner was the first service which focused its interest on author activity, developing specific indicators and grouping documents under the same name. Also significant was its provision of visual information and the presentation of multiple charts which helped users in the evaluation and benchmarking of authors, topics and journals.

However, the main reason why I consider AMiner to be a directory and not a search engine at all is that its search architecture is very poor. As indicated above, despite a platform focused on the author, the system indexes documents only. Thus, the profiles resulting from a query are displayed because they are responsible for the retrieved papers. This is a wasted opportunity to implement a true profile search engine that would allow a user to obtain curricula according to characteristics such as nationality, degrees, interests, co-authors, and so on – which would have made AMiner a serious tool for collaboration studies and demographic analysis of research activity. These searching problems are not only due to the difficulties in finding profiles, but also to the fact that queries are launched to a unique textual index where author, title, venue and year are blended. This results in a search tool which produces a significant amount of imprecision and noise, sometimes leading to a confusing and frustrating search experience. All this is accompanied by an inexplicable absence of search tips and a non-existent advanced search page, which confirms the lack of interest shown by AMiner's developers in establishing an appropriate and acceptable search architecture.

Sometimes, an element as crucial as the user's experience and satisfaction when using a search engine is not considered sufficiently important by its developers, who instead focus their attention almost exclusively on indexing, search features and ranking criteria. AMiner is a clear example of this: the web design is inadequate; pictures are poorly scaled; the structure is confusing and chaotic, with two menus that repeat the same elements or different labels that point to the same page; and the information is of questionable use, such as the term probability for each topic. Furthermore, important information such as the number of documents by topic or the origin of the data is omitted, graphics such as the pie chart in each 'Conference/Journal' page show incomplete results, applications such as 'Graph Search' or 'Reviewer Recommended' do not work, and so on. On the whole, it seems that AMiner is viewed by authors as a website which shows the results of their research projects instead of as a search engine that has to be sufficiently clear and transparent in its content organization to present valuable information on the overall database and its elements. Perhaps this also explains the limited usefulness of its search architecture, because the search function is the principal means of interaction on these types of websites. Thus, for example, 'Topics' is an element of the ACT model implemented by Tang's group, the purpose of which is to assign a topic to a document. However, this is not useful as a classification system because it is horizontal, with no hierarchy, and the terms are sometimes confused and duplicated (Monaghan et al., 2010). This disorientates users, who expect a thematic classification such as that provided by other academic search engines.

In summary, AMiner is an interesting tool as a source for scientific social networks analyses and to observe new indicators related to collaboration patterns. Its profiles are among the most complete and this lends it great power as a social networking tool and a Science 2.0 platform. However, and as outlined above, AMiner also displays important structural failures that undermine its value – its Achilles' heel being its search interface.

5

Microsoft Academic Search:
the multi-object engine

Abstract: Microsoft Academic Search is a development of Microsoft Research Asia which focuses all its service in the profiling of not only authors but also organizations, key words and journals. In addition to original visualizations and benchmarking instruments, this engine is one of the most innovative solutions in the scope of scientific information available on the web. Microsoft Academic Search bases its data entirely in the CrossRef database and employs an automatic citation index ranked according to the PopRank algorithm. Its principal weaknesses are its poor search mechanism oriented only to papers and authors, its suspect policy of citation assignment in organization profiles, and its slow updating speed.

Key words: Microsoft Academic Search, PopRank, Microsoft Research Asia, object-level vertical search engine, visual explorer.

Microsoft Academic Search (*http://academic.research.microsoft.com*) is a scientific search platform developed in 2009 by the Microsoft Research branch in Asia. Headed up by Zaiqing Nie, the main objective of this project was not only to be a specialized search engine of research papers, but also to be a global resource producing qualitative information about scientific dynamics at multiple levels – from individual profiles to research disciplines or academic institutions. In this sense, Microsoft Academic Search is more than a mere academic search engine that only returns data, and is set up as a web platform for research evaluation and the analysis and study of science in multiple facets. But perhaps the most relevant aspect of Microsoft Academic Search is its interactive dimension which facilitates users' involvement in suggesting the removal, correction and merging of data and profiles. This direct user participation, in which he/she is also the producer and owner of the profile's information, favours the reliability and accuracy of the data.

The origin of Microsoft Academic Search has to be considered in the framework of the commercial war between two search giants – Microsoft and Google – for the online global search market. In response to Google Scholar, Microsoft launched Windows Live Academic (WLA) in 2006 (Ford and O'Hara, 2007). Unlike its competitor, WLA did not crawl the web looking for academic materials, but acted as a hub that facilitated access to the main scientific publishers' platforms (ScienceDirect, SpringerLink, Wiley Online Library, etc.) and authoritative search services (CiteSeer[x]). It was restricted to computer science, electrical engineering, physics and related areas, gathering more than six million papers from 4300 journals and 2000 conferences (Windows Live Academic, 2006). Its search interface was integrated in Windows Live Search, showing only the abstract or full text of each record and providing the possibility of exporting these data to BibTeX or EndNote.

As with almost every Microsoft search service, WLA was a victim of the company's erratic policies with regard to their web search services, which are constantly removed or relocated to other places, and the names of which are frequently changed. In 2007, WLA was fully part of Live Search (previously Windows Live Search), finally ceasing its activity in 2008. In this way, the new competitor of Google Scholar failed almost at the moment in which it was born.

However, at almost the same time, the research division of Microsoft in Asia developed a prototype to implement its laboratory's research advances on the web. Libra was started in 2007 and contained approximately two million papers in that year (Libra, 2007), containing four-and-a-half million by the end of 2009 (Jacsó, 2010a). Unlike WLA, it contained a training database formed by bibliographic records from specialized web databases in computer science – such as DBLP, CiteSeer or ACM Digital Library. Libra introduced an important concept that would become a key element of the future Microsoft Academic Search: it classified and retrieved different entities related to the scientific information, not only documents but authors, venues, organizations and subject matter. Thus, it can be said that Microsoft Academic Search is the result of both Microsoft developments, because it contains the structure and functioning of Libra and the content criteria of WLA.

The object-level vertical search engine

Microsoft Academic Search inherited the structure and organization of Libra, or at least this can be deduced from the literature (Microsoft, 2011a). Microsoft Research Asia has not published anything about the functioning of Microsoft Academic Search, but it has made available several papers that describe the principal elements behind the working structure of Libra.

As indicated above, the principal characteristic that Microsoft Academic Search inherited from Libra was the assumption that Microsoft Academic Search was not just a web document retrieval system but a complete search engine of all the entities or objects related to scientific publishing. In this sense, Microsoft Academic Search takes into account the complex relationships between and among papers, authors, journals, organizations, and so on, and transfers this interactive environment to the search space, improving the search experience, jumping from one element to another, and, thus, obtaining an overall view of a research aspect in context. This requires a new approach when it comes to designing a search architecture, it being necessary to develop new ways of shaping the overall structure of the search engine.

In this context, Nie's team proposed an object-level vertical search engine (Nie et al., 2007b). According to this model, each object (i.e., article, author, etc.) is previously defined with their own attributes and elements (i.e., volume, number, references, etc.) to an article. Next, a focused crawler, accompanied by a classifier, tracks the web looking for research articles which are in PDF format and detecting the different objects included in them (Nie et al., 2006). These documents are then passed to an object extractor that harvests the attributes that describe each object. An object aggregator fits these data into a web data warehouse that corresponds to a real-world entity, for example detecting if two similar names could belong to the same author. Its objective is to integrate information about the same object and to disambiguate different objects between them. This disambiguation process is carried out via web connections and contextual information. Web connections refer to the fact that if two similar objects co-occur in multiple web pages, then the likelihood of them being the same object increases. On the other hand, each object establishes relationships with other entities, such as 'is authored by', 'published by', 'cited by', etc. These connections can then be represented as a graph in which an object – for example an article – is linked to several authors, multiple cited and referenced papers, multiple publishers and various subject matters. This context also helps the disambiguation process because objects that link with the same recurring objects are most likely to be the same as well.

Finally, the system incorporates its own ranking algorithm in accordance with the object-level structure. PopRank (Nie et al., 2005) is an adaptation of the PageRank algorithm (Brin and Page, 1998) that takes into account the relationship of an object with regard to other objects. As discussed earlier, each object is embedded in a relation graph in which multiple items are related in distinct ways. This enables each element to transfer its popularity to its neighbours, influencing the ranking of an object not only by its own relevance in the query but by its relationships with other objects. For example, the relevance of a paper is determined by the importance of its authors, the prestige of the journal or the value of the citing papers, as well as to the degree of similarity with the query. In this way, PopRank solves the problem of ordering different objects at an aggregated level and with different relevance criteria. This adaptation also comes from a critical perception about PageRank that it assumes that all the links have the same authority propagation factors, a questionable claim in scale-free networks such as the web (Barabási and Albert, 1999). Moreover, this assumption is even less secure in networks of disparate objects and different relationships.

Slow content updating speed

Microsoft Academic Search is one of the largest academic search engines, with more than 39.8 million documents and approximately 19.8 million author profiles, according to Windows Azure Marketplace in November 2013 (Microsoft, 2014). In a post on the Microsoft Academic Search forum (Microsoft, 2013), the engine's developers detail the sources that feed the Microsoft Academic Search database. A focused web crawl is carried out to extract research articles from web pages, then, in addition, Microsoft Academic Search indexes standardized bibliographic information from publishers (e.g., Elsevier and Springer), repositories (e.g., arXiv.org) and other bibliographic services (e.g., CrossRef). However, no information is given about the proportion of data from the web crawl versus the proportion of data from these other authoritative sources, as occurred in Scirus, for example. Perhaps the most surprising detail is the fact that the total amount of metadata in 2012 was 42 million papers, while one year later this had fallen to 39.8 million papers. This decrease could be the result of better integration of data, through a cleaning process to remove duplicated and erroneous records. Further, much of the metadata from the IEEE (Institute of Electrical and Electronics Engineers), the ACM (Association for Computing Machinery) and the AGU (American Geophysical Union) could be included in CrossRef already.

Table 5.1 shows the distribution of metadata and full texts according to the principal bibliographic sources. In 2012, metadata comprised almost all the indexed records in Microsoft Academic Search, which suggests that the proportion of web crawled data is quite low and is used to complete the existing metadata information. Looking at the metadata distribution in Table 5.1, CrossRef can be considered to be almost the exclusive source of metadata for Microsoft Academic Search, with 94 per cent. CrossRef (*http://www.crossref.org/*) is an organization devoted to promoting the scientific communication which brings together more than 4000 scientific publishers across the world. CrossRef is also responsible for assigning a DOI (digital object identifier) to earch article, a mechanism that makes it possible to locate and identify any article available on the web from participating publishers. This means that the metadata from this service are true to the original publisher source – making Microsoft Academic Search a totally reliable source for articles and journals. In addition, Microsoft Academic Search relies on access to almost 15 million full-text documents to extract abstracts and other contextual information, but this is not freely available to the user.

Table 5.1	List of sources that feed Microsoft Academic Search

Sources	Metadata	Percentage	Full texts	Percentage
CrossRef	40,000,000	94.23		
IEEE	2,300,000	5.42	1,800,000	12.12
ACM	80,000	.19	220,000	1.48
AGU	68,000	.16	111,000	.75
Elsevier			7,000,000	47.14
Springer			4,950,000	33.34
arXiv.org			680,000	4.58
BioMed Central			88,000	.59
Total	42,448,000	100.00	14,849,000	100.00

Source: (Microsoft, 2013)

Presumably Microsoft Academic Search uses the web crawl to locate open versions of documents already indexed in its databases from the CrossRef metadata or the other publishers' platforms. A matching process is thus carried out between the extracted data from the crawl and the existing metadata through the object aggregator. Elsevier and Springer are the two scientific publishers which contribute the most full-text papers to Microsoft Academic Search (with 47.1 per cent and 33.3 per cent respectively), while arXiv.org and BioMed Central are the only open access sources (contributing 4.6 per cent and 0.6 per cent respectively).

Almost 46 million (45,972,685) documents with a publication date were retrieved from Microsoft Academic Search, which is 15.3 per cent more than the data reported by Windows Azure Marketplace. The reason for this mismatch is probably not due to a date search malfunction, because different strategies return the same figures. The most probable reason is that some records may show erroneous dates or may contain several publication dates retrieved numerous times.

Figure 5.1 presents the distribution of indexed documents by publication date in Microsoft Academic Search. The plot line shows a very widespread distribution over time, with a soft slope that goes back to the sixteenth century. So Microsoft Academic Search could be considered a suitable source for studies on the history of science because

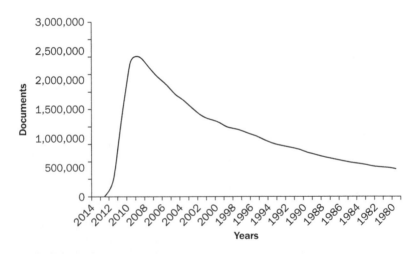

Figure 5.1 Distribution of documents according to publication date in Microsoft Academic Search

it is the most comprehensive search engine for historical scientific documents. However, 2009 indicates the peak for the most documents retrieved – five years ago. Moreover, only 8.8 per cent of documents were retrieved between 2010–14, and close to two-thirds of publications were published before 2000, which indicates a slight decrease in the indexation of current material. This is explained by a low rate of updating (once a year only) – the last update having taken place in November 2013.

Until March 2011, Microsoft Academic Search was a search engine specializing in computer science-related topics, then it became a multidisciplinary source that gathered from the widest range of research fields. Microsoft Academic Search now has a complete classification system which is structured around two levels. The first level groups fifteen general categories together, which are subdivided into further subcategories that vary from one category to the other – from the 24 subcategories of computer science to one multidisciplinary category. In total there are 205 subcategories (Microsoft, 2011b).

Table 5.2 and Figure 5.2 detail the distribution of the most relevant objects in Microsoft Academic Search by their principal categories. This classification scheme indicates the thematic coverage of the engine from different elements. Perhaps the most interesting observation is the high proportion of papers (18.9 per cent) and profiles (19.4 per cent) in the multidisciplinary category. It could be that this category gathers papers and authors which have already been assigned to other categories previously (Jacsó, 2011). In fact this is very likely to be the case given that the sum of the profiles and papers exceeds the total number of these objects in the database (Microsoft, 2014). Aside from this, the search engine has a significant presence in the traditional research disciplines – in particular, medicine, physics and chemistry are the categories with the most papers and profiles – with only a modest presence in agricultural science and environmental science. It is also interesting to note that the humanities and social science disciplines (arts and humanities, social science, and economics and business) are the categories in which the highest proportion of journals shows in relation to the number of papers and profiles, which indicates the wide dispersion of publication sources within these disciplines.

Table 5.2 Distribution of papers, authors and journals by research category in Microsoft Academic Search (25 February 2014)

Categories	Subcategories	Papers	Distribution (%)	Authors	Distribution (%)	Journals	Distribution (%)
Medicine	23	12,055,802	23.53	6,011,156	21.20	5,770	28.00
Multidisciplinary	1	9,682,253	18.90	5,512,004	19.44	358	1.74
Physics	11	5,011,189	9.78	1,854,981	6.54	738	3.58
Chemistry	18	4,419,051	8.63	2,838,421	10.01	856	4.15
Biology	12	4,134,882	8.07	3,102,724	10.94	2,273	11.03
Engineering	16	3,726,867	7.27	2,568,237	9.06	1,517	7.36
Computer Science	24	3,545,328	6.92	1,600,687	5.64	1,361	6.60
Social Science	14	1,898,433	3.71	1,048,870	3.70	2,246	10.90
Arts & Humanities	14	1,373,891	2.68	538,198	1.90	1,864	9.05
Geosciences	13	1,307,164	2.55	613,753	2.16	521	2.53
Mathematics	12	1,207,282	2.36	401,751	1.42	627	3.04
Economics & Business	17	1,019,032	1.99	512,850	1.81	1,428	6.93
Material Science	13	913,525	1.78	805,963	2.84	363	1.76
Agricultural Science	8	478,967	.93	445,221	1.57	326	1.58
Environmental Sciences	10	461,486	.90	504,324	1.78	358	1.74
Total		51,235,152	100.00	28,359,140	100.00	20,606	100.00

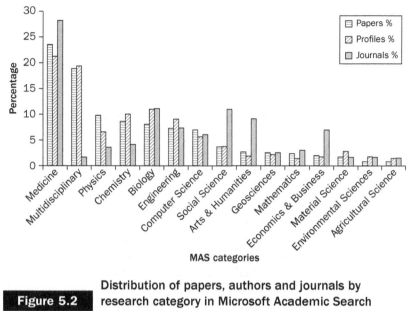

Figure 5.2 Distribution of papers, authors and journals by research category in Microsoft Academic Search (25 February 2014)

Filtering across the directory

Searching in Microsoft Academic Search is performed through a simple query box, as is standard in any search engine. Within this box it is possible to restrict the query to certain subject categories. The results display the documents that match the query and a list of profiles that also fit with the query. In addition, the left margin shows the number of resulting documents grouped by the main research categories, which allows the user to delimit the query according to those fields.

In general, Microsoft Academic Search suffers from a speed processing problem which was only partially corrected during the last technical update in April 2013. It is excessively slow when it comes to responding to the query petitions. One of the reasons for this could be that Microsoft Academic Search is an object-level search engine and it has to retrieve not only documents but all their links to the remaining objects, which could produce a high processing and consumption rate. As a result of these speed problems the system crashes frequently – and fails to show results. When this happens, Microsoft Academic Search displays the confusing message that no results in the database fit with the query, when at other times it does indeed show results for the same query. Although this message is clearly a means of covering up this technical problem, I think it would be more informative and more honest to explain simply that the system cannot support the query at that time.

Microsoft Academic Search also contains an advanced search that lets the user filter the results further, according to six fields: author, conference, journal, organization, year and DOI (Fagan, 2011). These fields can be combined in structured queries using SQL (Structured Query Language). However, they can only be linked through the AND Boolean operator by default, because OR and NOT are not understood by the system (Jacsó, 2010a). This causes problems when it comes to retrieving authors with different profiles or excluding terms for a query. The fields can be expressed using several tips – `title:`, `author:`, `jour:`, `year<>=`, `org:`, `conf:` and `doi:` – but the search interface does not support wildcards or other shortcut words.

However, a more conceptual problem emerges from within the search architecture of Microsoft Academic Search. It seems as though the search interface is not aligned correctly with the objective of implementing a search engine of entities rather than just documents. The engine presents a unique interface that retrieves documents and authors by default. But there is no corresponding information about organizations, journals or conferences. Thus, there is no specific search interface for each object, nor does the results page shows the different objects that match the query. For example, when one searches for 'England' the system returns documents with that word in the title, abstract, authors and venue, and returns profiles which include that name. But it does not provide a list of the journals and organizations – that is, the list of organizations that match with 'England' and the list of journals and conferences which include that term.

Similarly, when a subject category in the left margin is clicked, the objects listed do not correspond to the query, but rather to the retrieved documents on the right-hand side. For instance, and using the same example as above, if searching for 'England' and selecting the 'Medicine' category, there appear entities that do not have 'England' in the title, or that are not related to that country in the list of organizations, such as Harvard University. The same thing happens with journals and key words. So the left-hand side is a filtering instrument for retrieving documents rather than a section for displaying other objects that also match with the query. Using the advanced search does not solve this problem because when a query is limited via the organization or journal tip, the system continues to display articles and authors. It is only when a navigational query is performed – that is, when a user looks for a concrete journal or organization – that the system shows the specific profile of that journal or organization. But this generates a new problem, which is that the user has to enter the exact name used by Microsoft Academic Search for each search item. For example, there is no other way to locate the profile of the Universidad Nacional Autónoma de México – the largest university in the Spanish-speaking world – than to use the exact same presentation as here, because its acronym is not indexed and the search engine is sensitive to accent marks (ñ, ç, ö, etc.) and other specific spellings.

Thus, it is impossible to obtain a list of organizations, journals or key words that relate to a search query. For this reason, it is suggested that Microsoft Academic Search should change its search architecture entirely, indexing each object type in an independent index that can be retrieved and displayed in a separate section. Specific advanced search boxes would be recommended which would be able to return objects based on the different attributes that describe them, and not only by a matching process. These suggestions are made because, firstly, Microsoft Academic Search's search mechanism is not a true nor reliable object-level vertical search engine, and, secondly, this would make it a strong research evaluation tool that would easily benchmark different entities and enable the analysis of these data at an aggregated level. Improving its search utility in this way would help it fulfil the research evaluation tasks that would enable it to compete with traditional citation databases.

A multidimensional ranking

Microsoft Academic Search does not use a unique rank criterion because it retrieves several distinct objects which have different properties and, hence, can be ordered according to different criteria. In the Microsoft Academic Search forum (Microsoft, 2011a) the ranking mechanisms for each object type are explained. In general, query results within Microsoft Academic Search are ranked by two elements: by relevance to the query, and by a static ranking index. The way in which the relevance is calculated is unknown to me, so I can only suggest that a vector or probabilistic model is used that attaches a similarity score to each document with regard to a specific query. The static index is defined from the structural relationship of each object with other similar objects (articles cited by articles, authors that collaborate with other authors, etc.) and with different types (articles authored by researchers, papers published in journals, etc.). These scores are obtained using the aforementioned PopRank algorithm.

A composition based on profiles

Microsoft Academic Search is structured across six sections which correspond to the six objects involved in scientific publishing: authors, publications, conferences, journals, key words, and organizations. All these elements are interrelated and appear within each section, which facilitates the contextualization of the information, improving the interactivity of the system and the ability to search it. Across these entities, there is a 'dimension' subject matter, structured through the classification scheme, that cross-references the information of each object with its thematic classification, like a pivot table, allowing navigation across the search engine and mining deep into the stored data. For example, on the main page the objects are displayed in a horizontal menu and the classification scheme is displayed in the vertical axis, enabling data exploration by research disciplines and fields from the very first search.

Authors

This section describes via a personal profile the publishing performance of each author identified by Microsoft Academic Search. The author profiles section is one of the most complete sections in the engine, and the most unique when compared to other search engines (Figure 5.3). As discussed earlier, each profile is created from the metadata from CrossRef. This means that Microsoft Academic Search may generate several profiles of the same author if the author's name is written in different ways in the metadata. Thus, it often happens that one author can have two or more different profiles (see Figure 5.4). This is especially true in those languages with many possible name variants and different translations. In a sample crawl, extracting Stanford University's authors (34,709), duplicated profiles were counted: 5.7 per cent had the same name and 5.8 per cent showed as different ways of presenting the same name – such as Jennifer L. Aaker and Jennifer Lynn Aaker or Robert Abarbanel and Robert M. Abarbanel. I would estimate the duplicated

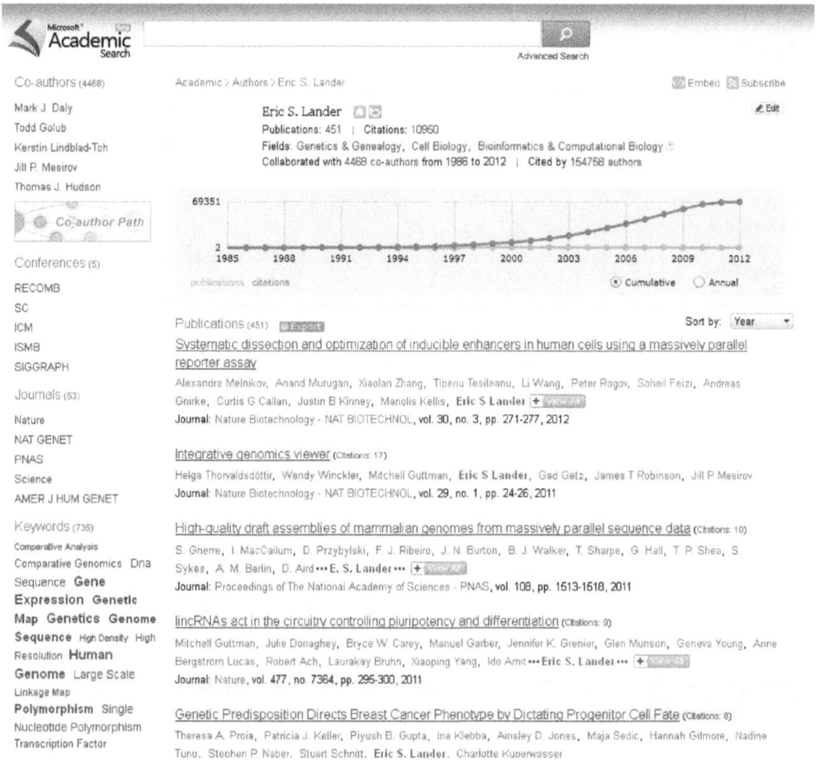

Figure 5.3 Author profile in Microsoft Academic Search (26 February 2014)

profiles to comprise 11.5 per cent of the total number of entries. However, this process was not exhaustive and only identified similarities within the sample; in reality this percentage figure could be much higher. Many of these errors are due to metadata mistakes by the publishers, and even more comprise old data records containing historical typographical mistakes extracted in an optical character recognition (OCR) process. However, solving these problems is critical because they arise often and affect the credibility of Microsoft Academic Search as a research evaluation tool.

As a way of solving this problem, Microsoft Academic Search allows users to register in the application, thus providing the option to change, merge and remove profiles. Through the 'Edit' option, basic personal information such as name and workplace can be edited, and links can be added to personal websites or research fields of interest. The publication

Figure 5.4 Example of multiple profiles for the same author (26 February 2014)

list can also be modified – correcting reference information and adding papers to an existing profile. It is also possible to merge two profiles into one. Other functionalities include the embedding of a profile in other web pages via a script command, and the possibility of subscribing to a profile to receive regular updates. Finally, the user can also add publications that Microsoft Academic Search does not list, by completing a form or uploading a BibTex file. These changes are not applied to the profile directly, as happens with Google Scholar Citations, rather the changes are sent to the developers' team to be moderated and considered. Although this provides more control over the profiles, avoiding the manipulation of profiles as happens with AMiner, it is unfortunately a very slow process. Sometimes one or two months (or more) can pass before Microsoft Academic Search accepts the changes.

The topmost part of the profile in Figure 5.3 shows the author's basic identification data, such as complete name, organization and basic bibliometric data with number of publications and citations. Prior to its latest update, Microsoft Academic Search also reported two bibliometric indicators such as the h-index and the g-index, but these were recently removed. This section continues with the research fields in which the researcher is included. These are assigned by a system based on the classification of the journals in which the researcher's papers are published and the number of co-authors and citing authors. These interesting categories can be also edited if an author does not agree with the categories assigned by the system. Next, the number of co-authors since the first published item and the number of times that the profile has been cited by distinct authors are shown. Further down, a trend graph indicates the number of each profile's papers and citations over time, both in an accumulative and annual form, as a way to observe the activity, experience, relevancy and impact of a researcher. Finally, the publications associated with the author profile and the articles that cite these publications are listed. Both the papers and the citing papers can be sorted by year, citations and rank (this last using, I assume, the PopRank algorithm). One other interesting feature is that the complete publication list can be exported using BibTex, RIS and RefWorks formats, which favours the interoperability of the records for curricula and other uses.

In the left-side margin, each profile gathers information related to the other objects in the search engine, a useful navigational interface that allows the user to jump from one object to another and explore their relationships. By clicking in the header of each section it is possible to see the list of items associated with that profile. Thus, 'Co-authors' lists the authors that collaborate with the selected profile and the number of partnerships, while 'Journals' displays the number of papers published in each journal by that author. The 'Citations' section contains the papers that cite the author's works. In this way, this frame shows the main co-authors, the principal journals and conferences where the author publishes his/her papers and the most representative key words that define his/her works. These key words are not extracted from the papers so it is possible that they are assigned by Microsoft Academic Search – however, the assignation process is unknown.

Publications

This section details publications linked to an author, key word, journal or conference. It shows the title, authors, abstract, venue and publication date. As previously, this list can be sorted by year, citation and PopRank. Clicking on each title, more detailed information is presented on each record – containing the essential data on the correct identification of a paper such as title, authors, citations, a descriptive abstract, venue information and finally the DOI identifier. This code is delivered by CrossRef and identifies each publication accessible via the web with a unique URL character string. Further down, the page displays links to the publisher's website or other services (such as digital repositories) to access the full text. So, Microsoft Academic Search acts as a hub that provides access to the papers' primary sources and their open access versions. In this way, Microsoft Academic Search makes it possible to upload the manuscript of these papers, thus also acting like a digital library or repository. Further, through 'Citation Context', Microsoft Academic Search extracts the sentences from the citing documents in which the citation appears as a means of contextualizing the meaning of the citation. This text comes with a linkable reference to the citing document and its authors. Finally, this section lists those references and abstracts contained in each paper that are also indexed in Microsoft Academic Search.

Microsoft Academic Search (2013) states that it groups multiple versions of the same publication together. However, one can see duplicated records from the same paper presented in an author's publication list which have been counted as different documents. These duplicated records could come from a different source; for example, one record could come from CrossRef and another from a crawl of open access repositories, or the record could have been uploaded by the author. Although this does not affect the citation count, because citations are always assigned to only one document, it can influence the performance view of an author, and other aggregated objects such as organizations.

Conferences and journals

This part describes the venues in which the papers indexed in Microsoft Academic Search are published. Both object profiles, 'Conferences' and 'Journals', present practically the same information. The only difference is that 'Conferences' also displays a geographical map provided by Bing with the location of the last conference. The first element in the profile is the title of the journal or conference – both abbreviated and extended which facilitates its retrieval. Next, the number of published materials, citations and self-citations, the publication period range and the fields of study are described. Also presented is a trend chart indicating the total number of published papers and citations in a cumulative or annual way. However, this chart can present several errors, and the described trends often do not correspond to the actual number of citations received by each journal in Microsoft Academic Search. In many cases the value plotted in the graph is less than that observed in 'Citation Count'. The same thing happens with publications, often showing a lower number than the actual number. Finally, the list of published articles sorted by year, citations and rank is displayed. As with the author profiles, the left-hand margin enables users to select the authors that publish most in that venue and the key words most used to describe those publications.

Table 5.3 illustrates the distribution of venues by subject categories. In general, medicine (with 22.75 per cent), computer science (with 19.25 per cent) and engineering (with 10.85 per cent) are the categories that present the most sources, while agricultural science (1.29 per cent) and multidisciplinary (1.42 per cent) present the fewest number of sources. By venue type, only computer science (73.98 per cent) and engineering (25.93 per cent) contain a significant number of conference publications – comprising 72.1 per cent of the total venues for computer science and 44.8 per cent of the total venues for engineering. It is not known why Microsoft Academic Search does not include conferences from other disciplines, in spite of there being research areas in which conference communications also have significant weight, such as physics, chemistry and geosciences (Lisée et al., 2008).

In total, Microsoft Academic Search includes around 22,000 journal titles. It is interesting to note that there are no article references to 2361 (10.7 per cent) of these, and 3819 (17.3 per cent) receive no citations. As for authors, it is assumed that the journal titles come from CrossRef processed references. However, the fact that journals also display the abbreviated title suggests that the title list is taken from a different source, independent of the article source. Moreover, the title abbreviations used are the same as those used by Thomson/ISI's Web of Knowledge, suggesting that Microsoft Academic Search has taken this journal list and then cross-referenced it against the CrossRef records. This would explain why there are journals with no papers and, therefore, no citations. An alternative explanation would be that the journal titles were extracted by crawling the web.

Table 5.4 gathers the ten most important journals indexed in Microsoft Academic Search according to the number of published articles. Generalist and respected journals as *Nature* (480,586 articles) and *Science* (290,013 articles) have the most published papers, followed by other specialized journals such as *Cheminform* (275,039 articles) in

Table 5.3 Distribution of conference and journal titles by research category in Microsoft Academic Search (26 February 2014)

Categories	Conferences	Conferences (%)	Journals	Journals (%)	Total	Total (%)
Medicine	2	0.04	5,770	28.00	5,772	22.75
Computer Science	3,523	73.98	1,361	6.60	4,884	19.25
Engineering	1,235	25.93	1,517	7.36	2,752	10.85
Biology	0	0.00	2,273	11.03	2,273	8.96
Social Science	0	0.00	2,246	10.90	2,246	8.85
Arts & Humanities	0	0.00	1,864	9.05	1,864	7.35
Economics & Business	0	0.00	1,428	6.93	1,428	5.63
Chemistry	0	0.00	856	4.15	856	3.37
Physics	0	0.00	738	3.58	738	2.91
Mathematics	0	0.00	627	3.04	627	2.47
Geosciences	0	0.00	521	2.53	521	2.05
Material Science	0	0.00	363	1.76	363	1.43
Environmental Sciences	1	0.02	358	1.74	359	1.42
Multidisciplinary	1	0.02	358	1.74	359	1.42
Agricultural Science	0	0.00	326	1.58	326	1.29
Total	4,762	100.00	20,606	100.00	25,368	100.00

Table 5.4 The ten most productive journals in Microsoft Academic Search (4 March 2014)

Journal title	Articles	Citations	Range years	Fields	Self-citations	Self-citation ratio
Nature	480,586	4,656,828	1869–2013	Multidisciplinary	90,439	1.94
Science	290,013	3,923,912	1880–2013	Multidisciplinary	8,513	0.22
Cheminform	275,039	46,601	1991–2011	Chemistry	7,647	16.41
British Medical Journal	247,453	544,688	1840–2012	Medicine	11,472	2.11
Lancet	233,249	1,402,807	1823–2012	Neuroscience	14,302	1.02
Physical Review B	207,344	375,907	20–2012	Condensed Matter Physics	1,336	0.36
Journal of the Acoustical Society of America	179,101	322,370	1929–2012	Natural Language & Speech	73,279	22.73
Proceedings of the National Academy of Sciences	158,959	4,075,221	1915–2013	Multidisciplinary	32,957	0.81
Physical Review Letters	151,585	712,614	1920–2013	Physics	1,290	0.18
Journal of Geophysical Research	142,360	1,739,751	1896–2013	Geophysics	587,509	33.77
All journals	35,527,602	212,003,471			16,717,933	7.89

chemistry and the *British Medical Journal* (247,453 articles) in medicine. The range years column presents some strange numbers – such as the publishing period of *Physical Review B* being 20 to 2012 or that of *Physical Review Letters* being 920 to 2012 – which could be mistakes in data capture. It is also interesting that only half of the ten most productive journals include articles up to 2013, even *Cheminform* only has articles up to 2011, which could be an indication of limited updating on the part of Microsoft Academic Search. In a crawl of the journals list in March 2014, only 2.9 per cent presented articles from 2013 and only 0.29 per cent presented articles from 2014. In addition, more than 50 per cent of the journals had not been updated since 2011, which highlights this search engine's poor upgrading. Furthermore, 10.7 per cent of the journals presented articles before 2005, some of which could now be considered obsolete. These coverage problems are in line with the early work of Jacsó (2011) on Microsoft Academic Search in which he highlights the incomplete coverage of specific titles. For example, Microsoft Academic Search has only gathered papers from *Library Trends* since 1978, when in fact this journal started up in 1952. Repeating this observation with three random journals – *Russian Social Science Review*, *Journal of Electrophoresis* and *Deep Sea Research* – it was found that the coverage of these journals was irregular, with important gaps between range years and ranges that were too short. For example, *Russian Social Science Review* has been publishing since 1960, all their papers are on the web and they have a DOI number, but its range is given as 2006–8. Although there is congruence between the actual range years of *Journal of Electrophoresis* and *Deep Sea Research* and the ranges presented in Microsoft Academic Search, the coverage within years is incomplete in many cases. To take the example of *Deep Sea Research*, Microsoft Academic Search only covers volume 24, issue 3 of 1977, while the remainder are missing; similarly, from volume 8, issue 2 of 1961, only one paper is extracted. The reason for this lack of papers is unknown because many of them have a DOI number and are hosted online in their publisher platform, and so are easily available and harvestable. Perhaps of most concern is that it is impossible to know for certain the number and proportion of missing papers; similarly, there is a real sense of arbitrariness in terms of why only certain volumes or papers are gathered. These errors and omissions are important because they could also impact on the other objects, providing an underestimated picture of author and organization profiles.

Table 5.4 also indicates that the total number of papers assigned to these top ten journals is 35.5 million articles, a little less than the 39.8 million documents at the last update (Microsoft, 2014). These additional papers could be conference papers (2.3 million) or other non-published materials such as repository pre-prints, working papers, books or technical reports. Perhaps another weakness of Microsoft Academic Search is the lack of classification by document types that would enable the user to know the exact amount of such material in the database.

Another interesting aspect is the self-citation counting. It is striking that *Science* – with almost four million citations – shows only 8513 self-citations (a self-citation ratio of 0.22) and *Physical Review B* – with 375,907 citations – only generates 1336 self-citations (a 0.36 self-citation ratio), while *Nature* – with 4.6 million citations – presents 90,439 self-citations (a self-citation ratio of 1.94). Comparing these results with other sources, for example SCImago Journal Rank (SJR) for the period 1999–2012, *Nature* shows a 1.5 self-citation ratio, not too different from the 1.94 of Microsoft Academic Search. However, *Science* shows a 1.33 self-citation ratio – very different from the 0.22 of Microsoft Academic Search, and *Physical Review B* shows a 29.6 self-citation ratio – vastly higher than the 0.36 of Microsoft Academic Search. This suggests a very different way of counting self-citations; a method which is unknown and which could fail to detect and process citations coming from the same journal. Perhaps the fact that articles and journal titles may come from different sources could explain why some citation counts do not match up with their corresponding journal.

Journal URLs were used to group the journals by publishing house or source. Table 5.5 shows the source distribution of the principal science titles. Elsevier and its online platform, ScienceDirect, represents 11.5 per cent of the journals, followed by Springer (8.5 per cent) and Wiley (7.4 per cent). However, these figures should be considered with some caution because some journals show strange links that point to Wikipedia, library catalogues or web pages other than the journal homepage. This happens with journals without articles, so it is possible that these journal titles were obtained through a web crawl, as was suggested previously.

Microsoft Academic Search also includes more than 5200 conference proceedings which gather more than 2.3 million communications – presented by acronym and extended name. There are 209 conference titles (4 per cent) that publish fewer than ten papers and 413 titles (7.9 per cent) that do not have any paper attached to them. And, when compared with Table 5.3 above, 9.2 per cent of the conferences are not

Table 5.5   Distribution of journals by source (5 March 2014)

Sources	Journals	Distribution (%)
Elsevier (ScienceDirect)	2,140	11.54
Springer	1,586	8.56
Wiley	1,377	7.43
Taylor & Francis	1,269	6.85
SAGE	547	2.95
Bentham Science	282	1.52
Emerald Insight	275	1.48
IEEE Xplore Digital Library	273	1.47
Inderscience	264	1.42
J-STAGE	260	1.40
All sources	18,537	

classified, or, at least, they cannot be retrieved using the subject classifications. As with the list of journals, it is possible that the list of conferences would come from a web crawl. The fact that most of these conferences show a link to the IEEE Xplore Digital Library (52 per cent) or the DBLP (24.8 per cent) suggests that most of the titles were extracted from those web databases. However, 4773 (91.8 per cent) of the conferences display a time period of which 78 per cent were held after 2000 but only 26.7 per cent were held after 2010. This shows an alarming lack of updating and devalues the significance of the information, especially given that the merit of a conference to the scientific community lies in its relevance, currency and immediacy.

Key words

This section focuses on the key words that describe the content of each paper. As was discussed previously, these key words are not the same as those included in the papers; they are assigned by Microsoft Academic Search, although the development team does not indicate how the key words are generated. Perhaps they are extracted from the main text of the papers, using some type of frequency criterion to obtain the most relevant words. The key words are then subjected to a stemming process to minimize duplications and to strengthen consistency and meaning;

however, some frequently occurring key words – such as 'case study' or 'point of view' – lack any significance in terms of content but seem always to slip through the net. Nevertheless, despite the presence of a small number of these insignificant words, the key words in Microsoft Academic Search show considerable congruity and stability.

The key words profile page shows the number of times that a key word is used to describe a paper and the number of citations received by those documents which include that key word. Next, the stem variations that encompass the word are detailed. As with all the profile pages, the key words profile page also displays a trend chart with the cumulative or annual distribution of citations and publications. As is the case with journals and conferences, however, these figures are very different to the counts given within 'Publications' and 'Citation Count'. A typical element of the key words profile is the 'Definition Context', which displays several definitions of one term that has been extracted from indexed documents in Microsoft Academic Search. However, these definitions are not very well refined and sometimes include erroneous descriptions of a key word due to stemming failures or the presence of synonyms. For example, 'genetics' is stemmed as 'genet', and then Microsoft Academic Search presents two confusing definitions related to computer science, far from the actual definition of genetics. However, these confusions are not frequent and in general the definitions are in keeping with the key words. It is clear, however, that not all the key words include a 'Definition Context' section because there are key words that do not have a clear definition – words such as 'large scale', 'empirical evidence' or 'real time'. As was seen with AMiner, these failures are common in search systems in which key words are extracted and assigned automatically, expediting the emergence of confusing terms and unusual assignations.

Table 5.6 groups approximately 58,000 key words by research discipline in Microsoft Academic Search (Microsoft, 2014). Clearly, these key words are often assigned to more than one discipline because the total number of key words by discipline is more than seven times the actual number of key words. It is interesting to note that the subject categories with the most key words are multidisciplinary (10.6 per cent), engineering (9.1 per cent) and computer science (8.9 per cent). Within the multidisciplinary category, broad terms that are used across all the categories (perhaps due to their low significance level) – such as 'large scale', 'empirical evidence' or 'real time' – are classified, which could explain why the multidisciplinary category features the highest number of key words.

Table 5.6	Distribution of key words by research category in Microsoft Academic Search (6 March 2014)

Categories	Key words	Key words (%)
Multidisciplinary	45,977	10.60
Engineering	39,473	9.10
Computer Science	39,010	8.99
Medicine	37,729	8.69
Biology	35,227	8.12
Physics	33,192	7.65
Chemistry	32,141	7.41
Social Sciences	28,348	6.53
Mathematics	26,736	6.16
Geosciences	24,902	5.74
Economics & Business	24,365	5.61
Environmental Sciences	24,033	5.54
Agricultural Science	20,380	4.70
Material Science	20,565	4.74
Arts & Humanities	1,864	0.43
All key words	433,942	100.00

Organizations

The organization's profile page is similar to the other objects' profile pages. It shows the name of the organization, the continent, the number of publications and citations, as well as the research categories in which it is active. The profiles of some large organizations, which are composed of other branches or departments, enumerate under the 'Sub-organizations' section the different units that make up the overall organization. For example, the sub-organizations of universities could be faculties, research institutes, hospitals, and so on, and specifying these helps to concentrate dispersed production within the same organization, also avoiding confusion in the assignation of papers.

Next, the profile displays the organization's URL and a map from Bing that presents its location, although this does not happen with all the institutions. 'Continent' is the only classification criterion that enables the grouping of organizations, but this is a poor and overly-broad criterion that does not permit comparisons between organizations from the same country or even the same sector. Even though Microsoft Academic Search expects to introduce a country grouping in the near future, it should also introduce additional classification criteria (e.g., sectors) that would enable the analysis of research activity at more aggregated levels, and between organizations.

As with all other objects, this profile page presents a trend chart of papers and citations that differs from the actual values in the database. It also ranks the list of authors affiliated to each organization, which can be delimited by the previous five or ten years' activity. In the left-hand margin, the most relevant key words for the organization are displayed.

Microsoft Academic Search uses a particular – and contested – criterion to assign citations and publications to an organization (Microsoft, 2011a). According to its developers, if an author moves to a new organization then their previous publications should be allocated in the new organization as well. Thus, new citations are computed both to the previous entry and to the new entry. This produces a distorted view of an organization's performance because there are some organizations that are counting research activity and impact that do not correspond to them, and the same information is doubled or tripled in aggregated counts. I had presumed that this assignation criterion was probably not taken from the papers' affiliations, but from the authors' profiles. Thus, when one organization changes in an author profile, the citations to that organization change as well. However, a manual inspection of a small number of examples confirms that the number of publications and citations in an organization is taken directly from the affiliation records, which are independent of the place of work on the author profile. For example, a search for the profile of a small organization called Oikon Ltd listed nine papers and two authors. But each author had only one paper in the database. So the papers belonging to that organization do not come from those two authors. Furthermore, looking at the author affiliations on the papers of both authors, Oleg Antoni works at the Ruđer Bošković Institute, Zagreb, Croatia, while V KU is Victoria Ku of the University of Arkansas. So why, then, are these authors assigned to Oikon Ltd? The answer is that Oleg Antoni wrote a paper with Sven D. Jelaska, who indeed worked for Oikon Ltd. And Victoria Ku has been confused with Vladimir Kusan, an Oikon Ltd employee. These confusions have originated in the parsing process, where, for example, the name of Vladimir Kusan is extracted as Vladimir Ku or V Ku, which then has been confused with Victoria Ku, and the affiliation of Oleg Antoni is confused with that of his co-author, Sven D. Jelaska. If the search for publications with "`org:(Oikon)`" is repeated, the results show nine papers, which is correct according to the organization profile, but most of them belong to Sven D. Jelaska. Something similar happens with the Emmons & Oliver Resources company (Emmons & Oliver in Microsoft Academic Search) – for which nine papers are presented from three authors. Two of the authors seem to be the same G.L. Oberts and Gary L. Oberts, and the third has been confused with another author. In fact, only one paper authored by these three profiles can be assigned to Emmons & Oliver Resources.

In addition to parsing failures when extracting names and disambiguation problems, mistakes occur because each paper is not assigned directly to an organization but has been previously assigned to an author, who carries the paper to his/her organization even though the article shows a different affiliation. This same thing happens with citations, which are computed erroneously.

Despite this, however, there are 4736 organizations (21.9 per cent) which do not show any papers, and 4967 (23 per cent) which show no author. Based on the assignation method, it is logical to find organizations with no author because there are orphan institutions where authors have moved to other organizations, creating the paradox of organizations with papers but without authors. This assignation method means that in order to find the actual documents affiliated to an organization, it is necessary to search using the search tip "`org:()`". However, this tip also retrieves the papers of authors erroneously assigned to an organization. Furthermore, the use of this tip would generate complex queries that would contain every one of the organization's name variants, increasing the searching problems already noted for organizations.

The high percentage of organizations without papers suggests that the list of organizations is also taken from an independent source – perhaps a web crawl given that all these organizations show their own web domain; and university colleges or research institutes belonging to universities are considered to be independent organizations simply because they have their own web domain. For example, the Faculty of Psychology and Neuroscience appears as an independent organization from the University of Maastricht, as does San Diego Supercomputer Center from the University of California, San Diego.

A counter-case to Oikon Ltd and Emmons & Oliver occurs with large and important institutions such as universities and sizeable scientific organizations. For these organizations, the number of publications and citations in their profiles could be much higher than in reality because they are also counting the earlier publications of new researchers from previous institutions and organizations. As such, a strange paradox occurs where new institutions, recently created, show publications from times previous to their existence. For instance, Paris-Sud University (University Paris XI Sud in Microsoft Academic Search) was formed in 1971 as a result of the division of the University of Paris, but Microsoft Academic Search shows papers dating from 1964. Another more remarkable example is the Charles III University of Madrid (Universidad Carlos III de Madrid in Microsoft Academic Search), which was formed in 1989 but which also holds publications dating from 1965 (see Figure 5.5).

Table 5.7 groups the top ten organizations in Microsoft Academic Search in terms of number of authors. In total, it gathers more 23,000 world entities spread out across five continents (Microsoft, 2014). Unsurprisingly, the organizations with the most authors are the big, state-level scientific institutions in large countries, such as the Chinese Academy of Sciences (43,586), the Russian Academy of Sciences (43,482) and Harvard University (42,435). However, the huge number of authors from Harvard and Stanford universities is noticeable given that their faculty members number 2400 (Harvard University, 2014) and 2043 (Stanford University, 2014) respectively, likewise the University of São Paulo with 5860 teachers (Universidade de Saõ Paulo, 2014).

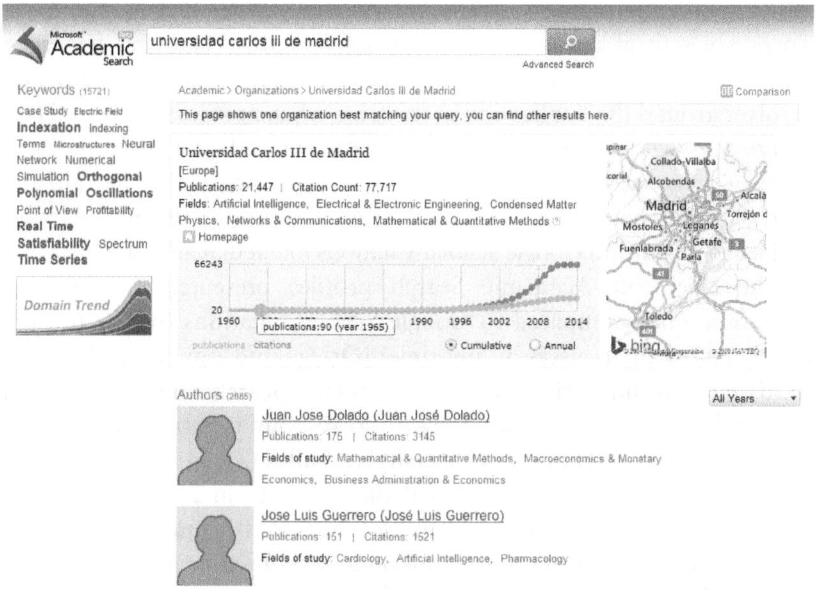

Figure 5.5 Detail view of the Charles III University of Madrid's profile in Microsoft Academic Search (7 March 2014)

Table 5.7	Distribution of the ten most important organizations in Microsoft Academic Search sorted by number of author profiles (6 March 2014)			

Country	Organization	Papers	Citations	Authors
China	Chinese Academy of Sciences	492,521	2,102,935	43,586
Russia	Russian Academy of Sciences	298,677	606,134	43,482
United States	Harvard University	598,801	9,336,939	42,435
United States	Stanford University	463,789	6,459,534	34,695
Brazil	University of São Paulo	186,362	747,557	32,136
United States	University of California Los Angeles	400,763	4,621,764	30,999
India	ERNET India	234,491	805,771	30,089
United States	University of California Berkeley	426,820	4,586,428	29,677
United States	University of Michigan	356,457	3,918,723	29,013
Canada	University of Toronto	329,250	3,545,927	28,835
	All organizations	67,952,682	535,873,602	7,532,038

There are several reasons that might explain this. The first has been discussed previously in the section on authors above (see p. 82) and revolves around the duplication that occurs when profiles are created (see Figure 5.4). The second is that the slow rate of updating could result in some authors showing their previous address(es) when they are already working elsewhere. A comparative study of profiles from Microsoft Academic Search and Google Scholar Citations found that almost 41 per cent of the Microsoft Academic Search profiles presented an outdated affiliation when compared to Google Scholar Citations (whose profiles can be edited by its users at any time) (Ortega and Aguillo, 2014). The third reason could be that Microsoft Academic Search contains historical data and these profiles could therefore correspond to retired researchers. A sample crawl of Stanford University's profiles (34,649) indicates that 21.9 per cent of its authors ceased their activity in 2000. Hence, the number of an organization's authors has to be interpreted as an accumulation of scientific staff from organizations over time.

Table 5.8 shows the distribution of the ten most important countries in Microsoft Academic Search, sorted by number of author profiles. The presence of authors from the United States is overwhelming, with

Table 5.8 Distribution of the ten most important countries in Microsoft Academic Search sorted by number of author profiles (7 March 2014)

Country	Papers	Percentage	Citations	Percentage	Authors	Percentage
United States	16,444,258	40.31	165,239,723	49.40	1,359,171	35.69
United Kingdom	4,496,422	11.02	40,063,095	11.98	357,178	9.38
Japan	2,955,287	7.24	17,809,855	5.32	237,488	6.24
Germany	2,044,290	5.01	14,373,657	4.30	189,418	4.97
Canada	1,767,801	4.33	16,135,383	4.82	165,767	4.35
China	1,474,244	3.61	5,913,095	1.77	128,981	3.39
Spain	815,744	2.00	4,528,882	1.35	106,483	2.80
The Netherlands	1,037,184	2.54	8,236,142	2.46	103,831	2.73
France	989,021	2.42	8,320,696	2.49	100,422	2.64
Russia	528,619	1.30	1,059,113	0.32	77,585	2.04
All countries	40,791,097	100.00	334,526,772	100.00	3,808,429	100.00

35.69 per cent. Far behind in second place is the United Kingdom, with 9.38 per cent, with Japan coming in third with 6.24 per cent. This distribution highlights the strong weight of the United States in the scientific community, followed by the European and Commonwealth countries. However, it also indicates the emergence of new scientific powers such as China. This arrangement is rather similar to other country maps based on Thomson Reuters Web of Science (formerly ISI) (Gazni et al., 2012) and Scopus (SCImago, 2014), so at a country level Microsoft Academic Search shows a balanced distribution comparable to other scientific databases.

Within this section, Microsoft Academic Search has a benchmarking tool that allows the user to compare the scientific production and impact of two organizations (Figure 5.6). This comparison can be made

Figure 5.6 Comparison of two organizations (7 March 2014)

according to research categories and subcategories, as well as by time periods (such as the last five years, the last ten years or across all years). Unfortunately, it is not possible to make a more general comparison of both organizations which would enable a wider assessment of their scientific performance. The top of the page displays two boxes into which is entered the name of the institutions to be compared. The resulting report shows the basic identification data of both organizations, such as: name, region, total number of publications and citations, the research fields in which they are working, and finally the ranking position of both organizations in that research field. A comparative trend graph then shows the evolution of both organizations according to the number of published papers and the citations received each year. Immediately below this graph is a list of the most representative key words for each institution – to highlight the research topics in which they are most prolific. Between these two columns, a third list selects the key words shared by both entities – to highlight the research fields common to both institutions. Finally, this page lists each organization's most prominent authors in a particular research field – ranked by field rating, citations or alphabetically.

Disciplines

Although Microsoft Academic Search does not consider research disciplines as an object, it does permit the grouping of objects according to its classification scheme, making this a navigational tool to access authors, publications, organizations, key words or journals in a particular research discipline or field. In this way, each discipline or sub-discipline ranks the classified objects by citations or field rating. In previous versions, these objects could be ranked by the h-index and the g-index, but these bibliometric indicators have now disappeared and have been replaced by the field rating. In its help page, Microsoft Academic Search (2013) explains that the field rating is similar to the h-index but is only calculated on the publications in a certain field. This new criterion, I think, is more accurate because the h-index and the g-index do not take into account the performance of an object in different fields, bringing the same value to distinct rankings. Thus, for example, a physicist with only one paper in the humanities would take first place in the humanities ranking because on average the global h-index of a physicist is higher than that of a humanist – which would thus create an unrealistic ranking of the most relevant authors in a discipline. Indeed, this failing is also observed in Google Scholar Citations, as we will see in Chapter 6.

So, each discipline and sub-discipline shows a ranking of objects that can be selected in the left menu. This list can be delimited by the previous five or ten years, and for 'Organizations' only a geographical classification enables the user to select institutions from five continents. These object lists only include the number of publications linked to each entity (except for 'Publications', which are ranked by citations only, and for which it is obviously not possible to group by publications).

However, it is not possible to know which papers within an object are classified in one or more disciplines. For instance, an author may be classified in several disciplines but he/she does not know how many papers are included in each category and how this affects his/her position in distinct rankings. This could be very time-consuming because if you want to locate a specific object in a ranking you have to browse the entire list until you find it, which could be a particularly protracted process when dealing with small journals or organizations. Perhaps the inclusion in the profiles of the position and value of each ranking would be an important datum about scientific performance in distinct research areas and would be valuable information for research evaluation. A manual inspection of several profiles allows us to determine this information without having to explore the entire rankings. So, the thematic classification is based on the journals in which the papers are published. Depending on the venue classification, an author or organization is thus classified in several research fields. In this way, in order to determine the position of an author or organization in a ranking it is necessary to know beforehand how the journals in which their papers are published are classified. Thus, the position of an object in a ranking is based on the total number of papers published in the journals assigned to that same category – citations being the aggregation of citations to those papers and the field rating being the marginal h-index for each research discipline.

Microsoft Academic Search established a limit on assigning research disciplines to an object: three for authors, five for organizations, and two for journals and conferences. These fields are assigned according to the number of papers in the journals classified in those categories, precluding categories with low representation. This is good for objects whose research activity is very much focused on a specific research topic, but it penalizes those objects with a multidisciplinary projection which disseminate their production across multiple research fields. Logically, this also means that the total number of values by discipline will not be the same as the total given in the profile.

Visualization: graphs as research assessment tools

Perhaps one of the most relevant aspects of Microsoft Academic Search is the incorporation of visualization tools that contribute added value to the search for and exploration of scientific contents in the engine (Bowen and Wilson, 2012). In this way, Microsoft Academic Search understands that the academic search engine is not merely a service for locating scientific data; it goes beyond this in its presentation of visual instruments that assist in benchmarking between organizations, in the monitoring of research field trends and in the analysis of collaboration patterns among researchers. All these functionalities are a good complement to the indexed data and add a new level of analysis that helps in the study of scientific dynamics and in the decision-making advice for scientific politics. The installation of Microsoft Silverlight is necessary in order to visualize these applications correctly.

Visual Explorer

This application is included in the 'Author' profile and it facilitates the exploration and visualization of the collaboration patterns of each author and the context of his/her scientific activity. This application also acts as a navigational interface because it allows the user to click on each co-author to see his/her profile or redraw the graph. Further, it contains several navigational tools that enable the user to zoom and move the graph along the screen. Within this functionality it presents four different data views: co-author graph, co-author path, citation graph and genealogy graph.

- 'Co-author graph': this shows a network from the 'Author' profile point of view, showing a scientific ego network in which the most frequent co-authors are located close to the author, while occasional partners are placed in the periphery (Figure 5.7). This ego view also shows the links between co-authors, making it possible to distinguish collaboration groups, the degree of betweenness, and, in general, the position that he/she occupies among their collaborators. This graph only includes the 30 most important co-authors.

- 'Co-author path': following on from the Erdős number (Wikipedia, 2014), Microsoft Academic Search measures the collaboration distance between an author and the famous mathematician Paul Erdős

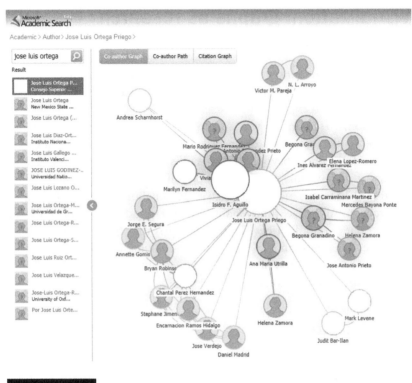

Academic > Author > Jose Luis Ortega Priego >

Figure 5.7 Screenshot of a co-author graph (8 March 2014)

by default, although it is possible to select another author as the final destination. It thus describes no more than five linear paths in the co-author chain that extend from the selected author to where the destination target is displayed, observing the distance between the co-authors that lie between two profiles.

- 'Citation graph': this visual shows the citations that an author receives from other profiles, 30 being the limit of citing authors in the graph. The distance of each profile from the selected author corresponds to the number of citations that each profile makes to the author – the closest being those who cite the works of the target author most. This view enables the user to assess the citation environment of a profile – indicating the co-authors most related to a profile's work – and to select specific papers from citing authors who mention the publications of the profile.

- 'Genealogy graph': this last view was removed from the lastest version of Microsoft Academic Search in November 2012 (Microsoft, 2012). The genealogy graph showed the links between advisor and advisees. This information was taken from researchers' homepages and described the intellectual influence of the Ph.D. director within their alumni. Perhaps this graph was removed because its use in current scientific curricula is no longer common as this type of relationship becomes more obsolete in a world where different types of collaborations and evolving research activity diminish the importance of an advisor.

Paper citation graph

This tool is still under development and currently is limited to 16 citations, a number rather low to appreciate a citation structure. This graph describes the connections that target papers establish with other papers through citations and, in turn, these citing papers among themselves, showing a citation network in which the intellectual influence between seminal papers over time is displayed. It also shows the context in which the citation is embedded, allowing the user to determine the significance of this influence. The distance between papers corresponds to the publishing time that lies between one paper and another – a historiograph that describes the evolution of this intellectual influence over a period of time (Garfield et al., 2003).

Domain trend

This visualization tool displays a dynamic timeline chart by research disciplines, with which it is possible to analyse the publication trends of sub-domains within a research discipline from 1960 to the present day. This interactive graph can be delimited by date range by selecting specific time periods, and specific sub-domains can be marked in order to observe their evolution, redrawing the graph by total count or by percentages. In addition to the graph, this application also shows a list of the principal authors in each sub-domain, which can be delimited by time range. This interesting application allows the user to study the evolution of different disciplines within a research area and its most prominent authors, creating a global picture on the historic evolution of a research field.

More a directory than an engine

Through this exploration of the functionalities and services of Microsoft Academic Search, we have seen that the main characteristic of this service is that it shows a modular structure composed of multiple key entities or objects involved in scientific production. Unlike traditional academic search engines which base their service on the retrieval of scientific documents, Microsoft Academic Search was the first academic search engine to turn its attention to the other agents that confer value on academic documents. In this way, the value or appropriateness of a document is assessed not only by its query relevance but by who has written it, where it was published, and where its authors are based. This perspective creates a balanced service where all these elements are presented and the interconnections between them are explored, making Microsoft Academic Search a complete service for scientific benchmarking and research evaluation at different levels. This contextualized environment also considerably enriches the user experience because he/she can navigate across different entities, jump from an article to its authors, and from these to their organizations, obtaining a complete view of the research performance at different points. In addition, Microsoft Academic Search incorporates various visualization tools that enable a complete and deep analysis of the data, analysing co-author relationships, citation networks and disciplinary trends (Hand, 2012). These applications enhance the search function, displaying processed information of relevance to research evaluation. All these functionalities turn Microsoft Academic Search into one of the most complete and comprehensive websites for scientific information and research evaluation.

However, Microsoft Academic Search presents some conceptual and technical problems that prevent it from being a reliable and precise research assessment tool because they introduce doubt on critical aspects such as duplicated profiles and citation assignations. Perhaps the most important conceptual problem is the unreliable citation and paper assignation criterion within organizations. This attributes papers and citations to organizations which are not responsible for them, resulting in questionable and barely reliable organizational statistics. The cases of Oikon Ltd, Paris-Sud University and Charles III University of Madrid discussed above are just three examples which discredit the use of this service for the benchmarking and analysis of organizations.

Further, duplicated profiles, which could total more than 11 per cent of the results, cast doubts on the individual evaluation of researchers because the production of one researcher could be distributed among several similar profiles. To solve this problem, Microsoft Academic Search introduced a mechanism to enable the changing and merging of profiles to gain greater consistency and reliability. However, some requests are either not attended to or take a long time to be resolved.

This leads us to another serious problem: the updating of the service is very slow in every aspect. Microsoft Academic Search has not updated its bibliographic records since November 2013. Thus, 96.8 per cent of the journals do not present articles later than 2013. Furthermore, the data updating is hardly ever carried out more than once a year. This provides a very static view of the service and leads to an inaccurate assessment of authors, journals and organizations. This lack of currency is a barrier to both research evaluation and information retrieval because scientific information is a very fast-moving environment where the data always have to be up to date.

Another limitation that undermines the value of Microsoft Academic Search, this time from an information retrieval perspective, is its poor search interface. It is incomprehensible that a self-named object-level search engine does not index and retrieve objects with a particular search interface, and then index each object in a separate index. Instead, Microsoft Academic Search only indexes metadata information from bibliographic records, retrieving only documents and author profiles. This would be acceptable if all the information about the objects came from these metadata, but, as has been discussed previously, the names of journals, conferences and organizations come from independent sources. This means that locating an institution in 'Organizations', or a journal in 'Journals', is a very hard task. This problem is made worse by not having a proper advanced search that selects records according to objects; instead, there are a couple of tips to delimit the document search.

Overall, Microsoft Academic Search takes an interesting approach that aims to represent the complex environment in which research production exists. Its originality is based on the independent description of each research object while maintaining the links between objects. This provides an interconnected space that improves user navigation and contextualizes the data. Nevertheless, its technical architecture, mainly its search interface, and the management of duplicated profiles are serious problems that undermine the power of this service and move it away from the main research evaluation databases. Despite this, I think that if these problems are resolved in the future Microsoft Academic Search could be a serious competitor to Scopus or Thomson Reuters Web of Science (Butler, 2011; Thomson Reuters, 2012).

6

Google Scholar:
on the shoulders of a giant

Abstract: Google Scholar is a specialized version of Google for academic documents. Through a massive use of crawlers and harvesters, it extracts metadata from the most relevant and recognized scientific sources across the web, and is one of the most up-to-date and exhaustive scientific information services on the web. Supported by Google technology, it uses a variant of PageRank to sort the documents and its own citation index to measure the impact of each piece of material. In addition to a main search page, it recently incorporated two new services: Google Scholar Citations (author profiles) and Google Scholar Metrics (journals). Its weaknesses are its opaque results, a poor search interface and the unstructured design of its new applications.

Key words: Google Scholar, PageRank, case law, Google Scholar Citations, Google Scholar Metrics.

In November 2004, in a decisive time of expansion for Google in terms of new applications and services, Google Scholar (*http://scholar.google. com*) – a beta search service – was born. This project was led by Anurag Acharya – a Google engineer who wanted to create a basic, free and supreme access point to the scholarly literature on the web for people all around the world and with any interest (J. Giles, 2005) – although it actually originated from the CrossRef project (Jacsó, 2010b). From this perspective, Google Scholar is considered to be the first complete search engine specializing in scientific information, harvesting research documents through a crawling process, and making available free access to the scientific literature on the web. In fact, the birth of Google Scholar was part of the expansion of the open access movement and it was a strong ally in the consolidation of this movement, making available open access journals, repositories and personal homepages as alternatives to the elevated subscription fees of the large scientific publishing groups. Google Scholar supposes a revolution for scientific information because it expanded the concept and source of citations, including materials omitted from other services, and provided an almost daily rate of updating. These advantages pose a serious threat to the traditional scientific databases which are now forging new developments and initiatives, as well as to new products that are following on this path.

A specialization of Google

Google Scholar is the only academic search engine that emerged from a more generalist service. To some extent, we can consider Google Scholar as a specialization of the generalist Google search engine and whose main functional and technical characteristics such as ranking and harvesting, and so on, are based on those employed by Google. In this way, Google Scholar begins with a crawling process to extract the appropriate information from seminal websites such as universities, digital repositories and scientific publishers to detect scientific documents under two basic conditions: 1) that these documents are scholarly articles; and 2) that they show a readable abstract. Thus, news or magazine articles, book reviews and editorial materials are excluded, as are documents larger than 5MB, such as books and long dissertations, which should be uploaded to Google Books and then included in Google Scholar automatically. In order to extract the basic information about each record it is necessary that these scientific documents include metadata that identify elemental information on the paper such as author, title, venue and publication date. Google Scholar supports several metadata formats, including HighWire Press, EPrints, bepress, PRISM tags and the Dublin Core format, with which it could gather a wide variety of documents. It also extracts information for non-structured documents such as PDFs if these meet a normalized structure. Google reserves the right to exclude any document if their identification data and references cannot be parsed properly. One limitation is that Google Scholar only crawls articles from a unique source, the authoritative publisher's site assuming first place. In this way, if a document presents several sources, for example a published article in a journal, with a copy in an institutional repository and with the manuscript hosted on the author's web page, the only source to crawl and from which to extract metadata is the publisher's web page because it is considered the most reliable source.

Perhaps one of the most important advantages of Google Scholar is its fast updating rate, upgrading mainly from new papers which can be added several times a week. The remaining papers are brought up to date according to the time required to re-crawl and the updating frequency of each website.

Feeding back its own sources

Google does not provide any information on the coverage of Google Scholar, it simply provides information about what kind of materials are not included, and claims that Google Scholar aims to be the most comprehensive academic search engine, harvested for metadata from scientific publishers, open access institutional and thematic repositories and personal homepages (Google Scholar, 2014a). Furthermore, it includes data on court opinions and patents. However, it does not detail what proportion these document types constitute nor the origin of the sources. There are no new studies that estimate the total coverage of this engine (Jacsó, 2005a). The most recent are the approximation of Mayr and Walter (2007), calculating the proportion of indexed journals according to different journal lists, and Aguillo (2012), who explored the coverage of Google Scholar through the hits per top-level domains.

A survey computing the number of hits per year was carried out to estimate the value of indexed papers. However, Google Scholar does not report the exact number of matches in each query and instead returns only a rounding-up. Unfortunately, it is not known how far this estimation is from the actual number; therefore these calculi are just a broad approximation. Searching year by year, the number of hits as far back as 1700 was extracted – this being the earliest publishing date with documents. The cumulative total from 1700 up to 2015 amounted to 94.7 million hits as at December 2013. This approximation is realistic if one takes into account Aguillo's (2012) estimation of 86 million articles in 2010. It should also be noted that court opinions, or case law since October 2013, are indexed separately to articles and that this legal material could approximate 14.5 million documents. In total, Google Scholar could contain 109.3 million documents, of which 94.7 million (86.7 per cent) would correspond to scientific documents and 14.5 million (13.2 per cent) would correspond to legal documents.

Figure 6.1 and Table 6.1 display different percentages because Figure 6.1 calculates the percentages over the total (including case law), whereas Table 6.1 calculates the percentages over just the articles. Table 6.1

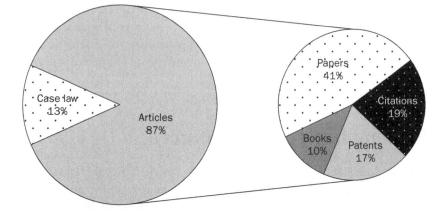

Figure 6.1 Distribution by document type in Google Scholar (7 December 2013)

Table 6.1 Distribution by document type in Google Scholar (7 December 2013)

Document type	Total	Distribution (%)
Academic papers	44,403,310	46.83
Citations	20,394,540	21.51
Patents	18,553,865	19.57
Books	11,467,605	12.09
Total	94,819,320	100.00

presents the distribution of documents by typology included in Google Scholar without the legal documents. The largest proportion (46.8 per cent) groups all the academic documents not included in the other typologies; thus, academic papers are research articles, proceedings papers, technical reports, teaching materials, and so on. The second largest category is citations, with 20.4 million documents (21.5 per cent) which include all the references extracted from Google Scholar's documents that could not be located on the web or that are simply not indexed by Google. Third is Google Patents with 18.5 million documents (19.6 per cent) and, finally, Google Books with 11.5 million documents (12.1 per cent). These percentages are similar to those of Mayr and Walter (2007), who suggested 28 per cent for citations and 53 per cent for journal articles.

Figure 6.2 shows the number of documents and citations in Google Scholar by publication year, and also shows the total number of both by publication year. The most surprising aspect of these longitudinal distributions is that they present a fluctuating trend unusual in other search engines. The results per year do not descend slowly, but instead chart an irregular pattern marked by peaks and valleys. There may be a number of causes for this, such as the heterogeneity of the sources used to index contents, or problems in identifying the publication date in papers with poor metadata information, or defects in the retrieval of the dates. As with CiteSeer[x], Google Scholar includes the citations taken from the indexed documents, which comprise 21.5 per cent of Google Scholar's total records. Excluding these, the distribution of publications is rather irregular, with the highest peak of indexed documents occurring in 2004 (2.6 million) and with 50 per cent of the indexed documents publishing between 1996 and 2013. These results suggest a slow rate of increase, with important currency problems. However, as has been suggested, the aforementioned problems with indexation and with the retrieval of dates would be the cause of this undulating effect. Another problem, as will be seen, is the inconsistencies between documents and citations because the system does not correctly distinguish between the two items, which results in the retrieval of erroneous data.

Table 6.2 illustrates the principal source types that contribute most to Google Scholar – the objective being to make an approximation on the

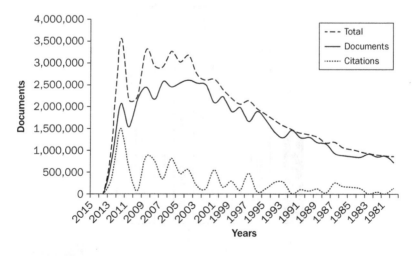

Figure 6.2 Distribution of documents according to publication date in Google Scholar (1980–2015)

Table 6.2 Approximate distribution of source types in Google Scholar

Source type	Total	Percentage	Articles	Percentage	Citations	Percentage
Publishers	30,822,200	41.60	28,711,300	58.84	2,110,900	10.42
Google Services	16,630,000	22.45	4,000,000	8.20	7,600,000	37.51
Thematic repositories	12,550,000	16.94	6,595,000	13.52	5,955,000	29.39
Institutional repositories	8,739,000	11.80	7,108,400	14.57	1,630,600	8.05
Bibliographic services	5,263,100	7.10	2,300,600	4.71	2,962,500	14.62
Online journals	80,500	.11	80,500	.16	0	.00
Total	74,084,800	100.00	48,795,800	100.00	20,259,000	100.00

significance of each data provider in Google Scholar. Successive queries about the most relevant publishers within the scientific scene were launched. In addition, a `site:` search was carried out to identify the hosts of these documents because Google Scholar locates the primary version of each paper (Google Scholar, 2014a). Before going any further, it will be necessary to explain the concept of the primary source and duplication control in Google Scholar. One piece of scientific research can be spread through a conference proceeding, a journal article or a manuscript deposited in a repository – all these being different versions of the same document. Taking this into account, Google Scholar groups these versions under a primary source, generally the authoritative publisher. This means that a document hosted within an authoritative source, i.e. a commercial publisher, could have different versions that are also deposited in repositories or referenced in bibliographic databases, but are not retrieved with the `site:` operator.

Overall, 62 sources were identified, representing 78.1 per cent of the records – 65.5 per cent of the documents and 99.3 per cent of the citations – in Google Scholar. Note that these figures are approximations given the lack of precision in the retrieval process and the errors introduced in rounding-up. The remaining 21.9 per cent of records could belong to the long tail of small publishers and institutions under national domains. Of the documents, 58.8 per cent come from online publisher platforms such as SpringerLink or ScienceDirect, 8.2 per cent come from Google Patents and Google Books, 28.1 per cent come from open access repositories or digital libraries and, finally, 4.7 per cent come from bibliographic services like the Institute of Scientific and Technical Information (INIST) databases or the getCITED.org forum (*http://www. getcited.org*). These figures are consistent with the results provided by Aguillo (2012), who proposed that 63.8 per cent of the records are hosted in generic domains like .com or .org, which suggests that these correspond to commercial and institutional publishers, while the 18.5 per cent from government and universities would correspond to open access repositories. Regarding the distribution of open publications, Mayr and Walter (2007) estimated this proportion to be 19 per cent; here it is suggested that 28.1 per cent of the records come from open sources, which does not mean that all these publications are open. Note that Table 6.2 shows only the primary sources, so it is possible that a considerable percentage of commercial publishers' documents could be hosted in repositories as well.

With regard to the citations, they come mostly from Google services (37.5 per cent), thematic repositories (29.4 per cent) and bibliographic services (14.6 per cent). The low proportion of citations from publishers (10.4 per cent) could be explained by the fact that the web platforms do not permit the accessing and processing of citations – that 10.4 per cent would correspond to citations from papers also uploaded to repositories as secondary sources.

Table 6.3 shows the most representative sources that feed Google Scholar, by number of hits. The web domains in the publisher column indicate documents hosted at those addresses which correspond to the name of the service in parentheses. It is assumed that documents under the .edu domain would belong mostly to institutional repositories or personal web pages where there is open access to academic materials, although this is merely supposition and the source type 'Institutional repository' might not be correct at all. Overall, Table 6.3 indicates that Google Books is Google Scholar's principal data provider (providing 12.3 per cent of its data), followed by PubMed Central (7.7 per cent), an open access thematic repository, with Google Patents in third place (with 5.3 per cent). Note that Google Books is a similar service to Google Scholar but specializes only in books, so it is very possible that it would contain materials from other publishers as well. Taking into account articles only, the principal primary sources are Elsevier (5.9 per cent), Google Books (5.4 per cent) and Springer (4.7 per cent). As with Table 6.2, citations tend to come from non-commercial publishing sources such as Google Books (37.3 per cent) and PubMed Central (21.9 per cent), which corroborates the previous suggestion that the publisher platforms do not provide citations to Google Scholar. It is interesting to note the negative value of citations from Elsevier (-40,000), which highlights an important inconsistency in the delimited search for citations and the anomalous working of the 'include citations' check. Citations are obtained from the subtraction of articles and patents from the total – the result of which would indicate the number of citations – because there is no other functionality that returns those data. Therefore, it does not make sense that Elsevier's overall total is less than the number of articles. These errors are not infrequent and they suggest a degree of caution when it comes to interpreting the citation figures within Google Scholar.

Case law

This specialist feature for case law was released in 2009 (Google, 2009). As the Google Scholar help page claims:

Table 6.3 Principal sources feeding Google Scholar (3 December 2013)

Publisher	Source type	Total	(%)	Articles	(%)	Citations	(%)
Google Books	Google service	11,600,000	12.3	4,000,000	5.4	7,600,000	37.3
ncbi.nlm.nih.gov (PubMed Central)	Thematic repository	7,310,000	7.7	2,830,000	3.8	4,480,000	21.9
Google Patents	Google service	5,030,000	5.3	0	.0	0	.0
Elsevier	Publisher	4,380,000	4.6	4,420,000	5.9	-40,000	-.2
Springer	Publisher	3,800,000	4.0	3,500,000	4.7	300,000	1.5
.edu (TLD university)	Institutional repository	3,340,000	3.5	2,560,000	3.4	780,000	3.8
Science	Publisher	3,180,000	3.3	2,960,000	3.9	220,000	1.1
inist.fr (INIST databases)	Bibliographic database	3,010,000	3.2	1,450,000	1.9	1,560,000	7.6
ieeexplore.ieee.org (IEEE Xplore)	Publisher	2,980,000	3.1	2,760,000	3.7	220,000	1.1
Wiley Online Library	Publisher	2,810,000	2.9	2,710,000	3.6	100,000	.5
All publishers		94,819,320		74,424,780		20,394,540	

> Google Scholar allows you to search and read published opinions of US state appellate and supreme court cases since 1950, US federal district, appellate, tax and bankruptcy courts since 1923 and US Supreme Court cases since 1791. In addition, it includes citations for cases cited by indexed opinions or journal articles which allows you to find influential cases (usually older or international) which are not yet online or publicly available.
>
> (Google Scholar, 2014b)

The origin(s) and source(s) of these opinions is unknown but we can suppose that they would come from a process of scanning, and other sources such as the law database FDsys (Minick, 2012).

The information is accessible through the 'Case law' section which is separate from 'Articles'. This indicates that the court opinions are indexed independently of the rest of the documents in Google Scholar, and in such a way that when a general query is launched, court opinions are not counted. However, this case law section includes court opinions *and* journal articles specializing in law. This is very confusing because these articles also appear in the 'Articles' section – perhaps a deliberate decision in order to avoid disclosing how many court opinions are scanned by Google. An unsophisticated approach would be to separate these data using the query "allintitle:'v.'" because the majority of these opinions include the abbreviation of *versus* (against) in the title. Clearly, this is not the best way to count these court opinions, but perhaps it is the only way to secure an approximation of this document type. In total, 29.7 million court opinions were detected, although many of these would be citations. Unlike the 'Articles' section, this section allows the user, through 'Select Courts', to delimit the court opinions within the range of the 106 state and 131 federal courts in the United States. The elements that describe each record are similar to those within the 'Articles' section, the only difference being that the page links to a scanned document hosted in Google instead of to an external resource.

However, this function has several limitations for a law-related user. Firstly, it does not include links to statutes and regulations that would enrich and expand the search; there is an absence of the context of each case and it is impossible to search for concrete document parts (Tarlton Law Library, 2014). Secondly, the legal opinions come only from courts within the United States; it would be interesting to expand these to incorporate historical opinions from other countries and include resolutions from important international courts, which would certainly help this resource to be seen as a worldwide tool.

Patents

Unlike the court opinions, patents do not have their own search interface and, instead, are mixed up with other document types which leads to different problems in the analysis of patent coverage. Within the search interface an 'include patents' check enables the user to estimate the size of the collection, as does searching for 'Google patents' in the publisher field of the advanced search. This procedure throws up approximately 18 million records (12.8 per cent), a long way from the 140 million patents apparently stored in Google Patents itself. This discrepancy indicates that only a fraction of the content of Google Patents is included in Google Scholar. Exploring the patent data within Google Scholar, it is clear that there are important limitations to the data and that only US patent applications are included (Hamilton, 2010). Google Patents, on the other hand, harvests patent applications from the European Patent Office (EPO) and also contains granted patents (Google, 2014).

However, the most important question is why there are patents in Google Scholar at all if there is a specific application (Google Patents) with a better search interface and broader coverage. Is this a deliberate strategy to supply Google Scholar with pre-existing resources from other Google services in order to inflate its scope? Perhaps the most rational thing to do would be to integrate both services with their specific interfaces and contents.

The opacity of results

Google Scholar's main homepage is very similar in appearance to that of the main Google search engine. It shows a unique search box where it is possible to specify the retrieval of research articles only (including patents) or case law from different courts only, because both document types are indexed and processed separately. This last option allows the user to delimit the search by federal and state courts in the United States.

The advanced search in Google Scholar presents the option of searching by all the terms, by the exact phrase, by records with at least one word, and by records without any word. But this type of query can be formulated using quotations, Booleans operators and shortcuts, without the need for an advanced search feature. Google Scholar also allows the user to search in only two sections of the document – the title and the body of the record – which does not offer any interesting options for limiting a query. Only three ways of filtering a query are provided: by author name, by publisher and by date. The search by author name presents some problems because this field is not normalized and depends on the metadata. Thus, it is common to find multiple variants of authors' names, in addition to instances where the search does not detect names in non-structured documents. This does not happen when searching by publishers because their names are pre-processed and unambiguous, although it is possible that documents from non-authoritative sources could contain important mistakes not only of publisher names but of author names and dates. Overall, the advanced search within Google Scholar is rather limited and presents few opportunities to filter the results (Mayr and Walter, 2007). It is very difficult to identify an author's publications, and it is impossible to locate publications from a concrete organization or country. Further, the localization of sources also presents problems in terms of whether the source is defined as a publisher or not. For instance, it is not possible to locate papers from PubMed because PubMed is not considered to be a publisher – in spite of being the third largest source within Google Scholar.

On the other hand, however, Google Scholar does contain several shortcuts which help to clarify its coverage and facilitate the locating of specific information that the user wouldn't be able to find using the advanced search. So, for example, the `site:` option enables the user to retrieve the principal sources that feed the service, and the `filetype:` option detects specific document formats (Table 6.4).

Table 6.4   Shortcuts accepted by Google Scholar

Shortcut	Definition	Example
`author:`	Searches in author field	`author:` smith
`site:`	Retrieves document hosted in that web domain	`site:` harvard.edu
`allintitle:`	Only searches in the title	`allintitle:` science
`filetype:`	Identifies the format type of a document	`filetype:` pdf
`date range:`	Locates documents into a date range	`date range:` 1990–1999
`~(word):`	Expands the query to synonyms of the term	~animal

In spite of the above, however, the search system shows serious inconsistencies that undermine the reliability of the engine (Jacsó, 2005a). It is important to bear in mind that Google rounds its results so that no more than 1000 records can be visualized. This practice alone introduces an element of doubt over the workings of the search system and the reliability of the search mechanism to retrieve precise information on a particular query. Further, it was observed that the total number of retrieved documents in a query changes as the user moves to the next page's results or selects a different number of results by page view. Another important limitation is that the date range simply does not work, as highlighted by Jacsó (2005a, 2010b). For example, the summation of five years (1970 to 1975) is not the same thing as the range 1970–5. So the use of this type of search is not recommended because the results could be meaningless. These inconsistencies emerge again when presented with the option of checking or unchecking the 'include citations' or 'include patents' fields. As was explained in the coverage section above (see p. 111), sometimes the total number of records is less than the filtered search excluding citations or patents. The same happens with the use of Boolean operators which return inexact numbers, as when, for example, the OR operator sometimes delimits a query instead of expanding it (Jacsó, 2008b). All these issues foster a deep mistrust over the reliability of Google Scholar's results and, above all, over its utility as an academic search engine for research evaluation – an issue of critical importance for the scientific community.

Unlike Microsoft Academic Search or AMiner, the Google Scholar results page links directly to the requested resource. Therefore the results page displays all the information that Google Scholar gathers for each document (Figure 6.3). Figure 6.3 displays only ten results by page – which can be expanded up to 20 results. This is a rather limited number of records per page, which could make the analysis of results a tedious task, especially when a query returns thousands of documents.

In the main part of the page the title of the resource, the authors, the venue, the publication date and source are presented. Next, a brief abstract extracted from the text is displayed which contextualizes the search terms in the results. Directly underneath, the number of times that that resource is cited in Google Scholar is given, with a link to those citing papers. 'Related articles' provides the option to retrieve papers with similar titles. Next to this, Google Scholar groups the different versions of the same document that its bots locate from across the web. This feature could make Google Scholar the best academic search engine for the identification and control of duplicated records – grouping

Figure 6.3 Results page of Google Scholar (15 March 2014)

Note: Google and the Google logo are registered trademarks of Google Inc., used with permission

similar documents as different versions of the same record, the authoritative publisher being the primary version indexed. Next, the service lists the most frequent styles used to cite the resource – such as the Modern Language Association (MLA), the American Psychological Association (APA) and the Chicago Manual of Style – and facilitates export to the most extended reference manager tools such as EndNote, Reference Manager or RefWorks. To use this exporting device, it is necessary to have saved the record previously in a personal bibliographic database ('My library') emulating a reference management tool. Finally, in the right-hand margin, Google Scholar displays links to the full text where open in a repository or if provided by the user's institution's library. In this way, Google Scholar connects its results with the link resolver (e.g., SFX, 360 Link, LinkSource) of the user's institution's library which is identified by an IP address range. Thus, if Google Scholar is used on a university computer a link would be provided to the university's library if it is a subscriber to that document.

The left-hand margin contains different search tools to delimit the results. Thus, 'Articles' can be selected if searching for scientific papers or 'Case law' if searching for court opinions. Within the 'Any time' tool, it is possible to delimit the query to only those records from a specific date or range. This could be used to split results from broad queries with more than a thousand results. Below this, two sorting criteria are presented: by relevance, which is based on the PageRank algorithm, and by date, which ranks the results by the date on which the records were harvested from the web. Next, two checks allow the user to select whether the results are to include patents and citations – but this does not allow the user to search only patents or citations. Finally, an alert can be created for new updates.

Data consistency

For some time now, several studies have pointed to Google Scholar's poor data consistency, principally in the areas of duplication management, the accuracy of document parsing and erroneous citation counting and assignation (Bar-Ilan, 2008; Jacsó, 2008b). Many of these inconsistencies have been resolved. Thus, different versions of the same paper are now successfully grouped under the 'versions' link; the extraction of authors, venues and titles from metadata has been corrected and it is now difficult to find anomalous authors such as 'I. Introduction' or dates such as '601'. However, problems regarding the citations persist. To take a representative bibliometric paper 'An index to quantify an individual's scientific research output' by Jorge Hirsch, published in 2005 in *Proceedings of the National Academy of Sciences*, Google Scholar retrieves 3745 citations, but a year-by-year search returns 3692 citations – 1.5 per cent fewer. This is probably a search problem, rather than an incorrect citation count. Nonetheless, 14 citations come from papers published before 2005, indeed many of them do not really cite the article at all. Although this margin of error is low in relation to the total number of citations, these incorrect assignations might be significant in terms of the research evaluation process.

Ranking

Perhaps one of the characteristics that identifies Google most clearly and distinguishes it from other search services is its ranking algorithm, PageRank – a key element in the success of Google as a search engine (Brin and Page, 1998). This algorithm assumes that not all web pages have the same probability of being reached by a random surfer. Pages with a high number of links have a greater likelihood of being reached than those with few connections. In addition, the algorithm introduces the idea that not all links carry the same weight, and links from a popular site with many incoming links are more important than a link from a barely connected page. Hence, PageRank derives from the Markov chain in which one page transfers its PageRank value to another page through its links. To summarize, the value of a page is defined by the number of in-links and the importance, in turn, of the linking pages.

Obviously, Google Scholar also implements the PageRank algorithm in its results but adapts it to the research production environment. So, links are converted to citations and other variables are added, such as venue and author. In this way, the first results in a query are those that are much cited and whose citations come from prestigious articles that also carry an important amount of citations. Articles authored by highly-cited authors and published in journals with an elevated impact factor are also considered in the relevance of a paper. A study on ranking criteria found that the main ranking criterion in Google Scholar is citations, followed by author name and venue. It also found that the algorithm changes if it is searching in the full text or in the title, and that it does not weight the term occurrence frequency in the text (Beel and Gipp, 2009).

Google Scholar's additional services

Google Scholar is a search engine with no sections or parts, unlike Microsoft Academic Search or AMiner. Thus it is only possible to mention Google Scholar Citations and Google Scholar Metrics as two recent services added to Google Scholar which have their own identity but which are not well integrated within its fundamental structure – which betrays a certain amount of improvization and the absence of preconceived functionality and planning.

Google Scholar Citations

One of the most recent functions is Google Scholar Citations, an application that enables the design of a personal curriculum from the data within Google Scholar. This feature was first presented in April 2011, to invited testers (Google Scholar Blog, 2011a), and in November 2011 it was opened up to the entire researcher community (Google Scholar Blog, 2011b). Until that time, Microsoft Academic Search and AMiner were the only academic search services that displayed the personal profiles of researchers, therefore it is reasonable to suppose that this new Google Scholar application was a response to those initiatives, especially when Microsoft Academic Search became a multidisciplinary engine (Fenner, 2011; Aguillo, 2012).

However, Google Scholar's approach was unlike those other profile developments – within Google Scholar Citations there is no previous profile definition, instead this is filled out by the users themselves, enabling them to edit the contents of a profile freely. To access their own profile, users simply need to be registered with Google. Then they can fill out each field with whatever information they consider important. Next they can select their own publications indexed by Google Scholar. Finally, Google Scholar Citations calculates the citations for these selected papers, and several other bibliometric indicators that are incorporated within the profile, and then the information can be used to rank one author alongside other authors. The principal advantage of this approach is that the users are the ultimate owner of the profile, editing when they want and with the information that they desire, selecting, merging and removing publications from their profile. This provides current and appropriate profiles that correspond to the users' research activity because they include those publications that are available in Google Scholar and that belong to their body of work. However, this freedom can also lead to the intentional manipulation of profiles and the adoption of unethical practices (Delgado López-Cozar et al., 2012), as, for example, in the creation of multiples profiles of the same author (see, for example, Albert Einstein), or in the erroneous assignation of papers, or in the addition of prestigious researchers as co-authors. Another significant problem arises within the data mining and processing because each profile is written in the author's own language, which increases the incidence of, for example, similar words in different languages, misspellings and multiple name variants of the same organization. This requires a greater effort in cleaning data to obtain representative information on organizational affiliations and research interests, and so on.

In the case of Google Scholar Citations, the service is poorly integrated within Google Scholar, and access to it is difficult. Author profiles are located by launching a general query in Google Scholar which within the results, at the top, returns profiles that match the query, reporting a maximum of only three profiles. Alternatively, one can launch a query and click on the author name of any records that are underlined, indicating which authors have a profile. However, when a profile is accessed, a search box appears on the right-hand side in which it is possible to search only the information included in the profile (Figure 6.4). Thus, Google Scholar Citations provides its own search box for locating profiles,

Theodor Adorno

Sociology, Frankfurt School
sociology
No verified email
Homepage

Google scholar

Search Authors

Get my own profile - Help

Follow this author
1 Follower

Follow new articles
Follow new citations

Co-authors
No co-authors

Citation indices		
	All	Since 2009
Citations	95778	33677
h-index	116	71
i10-index	383	280

Citations to my articles

Show: 20 ▾ 1-20 Next >

Title / Author	Cited by	Year
The authoritarian personality TW Adorno, E Frenkel-Brunswik, DJ Levinson New York	11124	1950
Dialectic of enlightenment: Philosophical fragments M Horkheimer, TW Adorno, GS Noerr Stanford Univ Pr	9415 *	2002
Kulturindustrie. Aufklärung als Massenbetrug M Horkheimer, TW Adorno Dialektik der Aufklärung. Philosophische Fragmente, Frankfurt 128, 176	6379 *	1969
Dialektik der Aufklärung M Horkheimer, TW Adorno S. Fischer	5862 *	1969
Minima moralia: reflexões a partir da vida danificada TW Adorno Ática	3811 *	1992
Minima moralia: reflecţii dintr-o viaţă mutilată TW Adorno Grupul Ed. Art	3807 *	2007
Minima moralia: reflexiones desde la vida dañada TW Adorno Akal Ediciones Sa	3806	2004
Minima moralia: reflektioner fra det beskadigede liv TW Adorno Gyldendal	3802 *	2003
Dialética do esclarecimento T Adorno, M Horkheimer Rio de Janeiro: Jorge Zahar 45, 53-112	3310	1985

Figure 6.4 **Personal profile within Google Scholar Citations (10 March 2014)**

Note: Google and the Google logo are registered trademarks of Google Inc., used with permission

indexing data from the author's name, affiliation, labels and email address. This search box does not provide an advanced search but it does allow the use of certain tips to locate specific information included in the profiles. For example, the tip `label:` retrieves all the authors that contain the search terms in their personal interests, and `author:` searches only within the author's name. No further tips have been found because the help page does not deliver any information about them. So, search functionality is quite poor, with only a few shortcuts and a lack of structural indexing and advanced retrieval. For example, the function does not allow the user to select authors from a specific institution or country, rendering it useless for aggregated studies at a country or institutional level, without first having to carry out a cleaning and normalizing process (Ortega and Aguillo, 2013). Nor is it possible to search for documents or co-authors in an author's profile, which constitutes a serious limitation in terms of processing and analysing that information. Finally, profiles are ranked by the total number of citations that they receive.

Each profile contains an identification element in which the user inputs the full name of the profile, the working address, certain labels or key words and an email contact address and personal homepage. It is also possible to upload a recent photograph. Below this, an indicator section provides the scientific performance of each profile, essentially based on three indicators: citations, the h-index and the i10-index. This last indicator is the brainchild of Google Scholar Citations and simply measures the number of papers with more than ten citations. These indicators are calculated in two columns representing the total number and the number over the last five years, the latter being a way to assess the performance of an author over his/her last five years, indicating whether he/she is a young researcher with a budding career or a senior academic with extensive experience. Next to this table, Google Scholar Citations displays a bar chart showing the longitudinal evolution of received citations to the profile's papers. Next, publications included in Google Scholar and authored by the profile are listed. Twenty default documents are shown, although up to 100 records can be listed. Each entry displays the basic identification data (title, author and venue), number of citations and publication date, and the data can be sorted by those three criteria. Finally, on the right-hand side, Google Scholar Citations presents certain functionalities such as the aforementioned search box and the search alerts that inform the user of new articles and new citations to a certain profile. In this section it is also possible to search and link the profiles of co-authors, which acts as a navigational tool for searching profiles and documents.

Clicking in the title of each document, Google Scholar Citations provides further, more detailed information on the record, presenting a complete bibliographic description of the document. Moreover, the information on the number of citations links to a query in Google Scholar and retrieves all the publications that cite that document. Below this, a citation graph is displayed, similar to that shown in Figure 6.4, but this time it only includes the specific citations to that document. Further down the page are listed the various existing versions of that document – such as different editions and language translations of the same work, hosted manuscripts or pre-prints in open access repositories. Finally, exporting options are displayed – BibTeX, EndNote, Reference Manager and CSV (comma-separated values) being the available formats.

Since December 2011 several crawling processes have been run to assess the coverage of this service (Ortega and Aguillo, 2012, 2013). Firstly, 600 random queries were built by combining the 26 letters of the Latin alphabet in groups (strings) of two (that is, aa, ab, ac, and so on). These were then automatically launched to the search engine and the resulting profiles from these queries were retrieved and stored. Secondly, that very exhaustive list of profiles was then used to harvest author information such as working address, email domain, bibliometric indicators (papers, citations, the h-index and the i10-index) and a list of co-authors. Using this method, 296,205 profiles were detected, which allows us to make an approximate estimation of 350,000 profiles in Google Scholar Citations at December 2013 through a capture–re-capture formula (Ortega and Aguillo, 2012). A total of 18.3 million papers from Google Scholar were assigned to these 296,205 profiles, therefore it is possible that more than 56 million documents (76.4 per cent) do not yet belong to a profile. This could be an indicator of both the relative youth and growth power of this service which was created in 2011.

Table 6.5 describes the distribution of the ten countries with the most profiles in Google Scholar Citations (the nationality of each profile was detected for 88.5 per cent of the sample). The countries with the highest number of author profiles are the United States (24.8 per cent), the United Kingdom (6.4 per cent) and Brazil (5.2 per cent). It is interesting to note the strong presence of Brazil, while highly-scientific countries such as China and Japan are not represented in this top ten countries' list. Unlike Microsoft Academic Search and other bibliographic databases, profiles in Google Scholar Citations are created by the author him-/herself which could result in a significant bias in favour of those countries or institutions with a better or higher contact with this service, and in favour of those authors interested in maintaining an online profile. As such, these data indicate that there is a massive colonization of Brazilian researchers within Google Scholar Citations, while Chinese and Japanese researchers appear to be less interested in the service.

Table 6.6 reinforces the data observed previously in Table 6.5. Three of the four organizations with the most profiles are Brazilian: Universidade de São Paulo (1.3 per cent), Universidade Estadual Paulista (0.6 per cent) and Universidade Estadual de Campinas (0.4 per cent). This suggests that the service is populated by a high proportion of researchers from Brazilian institutions. We also find those organizations most often present in research rankings, such as the University of Michigan (0.5 per cent),

Table 6.5 Distribution of the ten countries with the most profiles in Google Scholar Citations (December 2013)

Country	Papers	Distribution (%)	Citations	Distribution (%)	Profiles	Distribution (%)
United States	3,335,218	44.7	86,980,173	57.6	46,503	24.8
United Kingdom	830,048	11.1	18,980,496	12.6	12,079	6.4
Brazil	516,272	6.9	4,324,713	2.9	9,734	5.2
Australia	451,480	6.0	7,057,002	4.7	6,161	3.3
Canada	364,036	4.9	8,098,539	5.4	5,705	3.0
Italy	421,866	5.7	6,500,631	4.3	5,594	3.0
The Netherlands	258,220	3.5	4,704,472	3.1	3,624	1.9
Spain	180,928	2.4	2,241,782	1.5	3,107	1.7
Germany	166,470	2.2	3,078,597	2.0	3,077	1.6
Malaysia	106,005	1.4	423,089	0.3	3,005	1.6
All countries	7,466,454	100.0	151,043,150	100.0	187,301	100.0

Table 6.6 Distribution of the ten organizations with the most profiles in Google Scholar Citations (December 2013)

Country	Organization	Papers	(%)	Citations	(%)	Profiles	(%)
Brazil	Universidade de São Paulo	210,005	1.1	1,929,059	0.6	3,764	1.3
Brazil	Universidade Estadual Paulista	87,696	0.5	470,275	0.1	1,636	0.6
United States	University of Michigan	114,933	0.6	3,209,638	1.0	1,581	0.5
Brazil	Universidade Estadual de Campinas	67,438	0.4	616,300	0.2	1,320	0.4
United States	Harvard University	90,440	0.5	4,938,666	1.5	1,205	0.4
United States	University of Washington	73,862	0.4	2,406,413	0.7	1,193	0.4
France	CNRS	113,782	0.6	2,177,599	0.7	1,185	0.4
United States	University of Maryland	78,774	0.4	2,120,427	0.6	1,146	0.4
United States	University of Minnesota	73,537	0.4	1,976,899	0.6	1,117	0.4
United States	University of Illinois at Urbana-Champaign	60,137	0.3	1,442,494	0.4	1,044	0.4
	All organizations	18,341,461	100.0	330,098,598	100.0	296,205	100.0

Harvard University (0.4 per cent) and the University of Washington (0.4 per cent). This unusual distribution is a symptom of the aforementioned fact that these profiles are created by their own users and therefore are influenced by the way in which this new product is disseminated among the scholarly community, following a similar pattern to the spread of information, disease or innovations in social networks (Valente, 2010). But this also raises important questions about the coverage of the profiles because it is not homogeneous and, as in the Brazilian case, can lead to a massive presence of profiles from a specific institution or a specific country, which could provide a distorted and unrealistic view of the service.

According to the thematic distribution of the profiles, the labels used by each researcher to describe his/her research activity can be a suitable proxy that would enable the user to observe the disciplinary areas in which researchers carry out their work. A total of 521,397 labels were extracted from the user profiles. Table 6.7 presents the ten labels used most frequently to describe the interests of the scientists that inhabit Google Scholar Citations. The most frequent key words are 'machine learning' (4661 uses), 'artificial intelligence' (4176 uses) and 'computer vision' (3219 uses) – all belonging to the field of computer science. In fact, 'ecology' (1714 uses) and 'neuroscience' (1620 uses) are the only labels not related to the computing environment. This indicates that the

Table 6.7   **Frequency of the ten most-used labels in Google Scholar Citations**

Label	Frequency
Machine learning	4,661
Artificial intelligence	4,176
Computer vision	3,219
Bioinformatics	2,827
Data mining	2,060
Software engineering	1,716
Ecology	1,714
Image processing	1,662
Robotics	1,621
Neuroscience	1,620
All labels	521,397

majority of users of Google Scholar Citations are closely involved with the disciplines of computer science and information science, and perhaps that they are colonizing this platform due to their proximity to and familiarity with these information technologies and web-related surroundings. On the other hand, the absence of labels related to relevant scientific fields such as medicine, chemistry and physics is surprising. This subject matter pattern was also detected in an earlier study on data from December 2011, where the high proportion of computer science and biology labels was evident while labels related to the fields of medicine or chemistry were minimal (Ortega and Aguillo, 2012) (Figure 6.5).

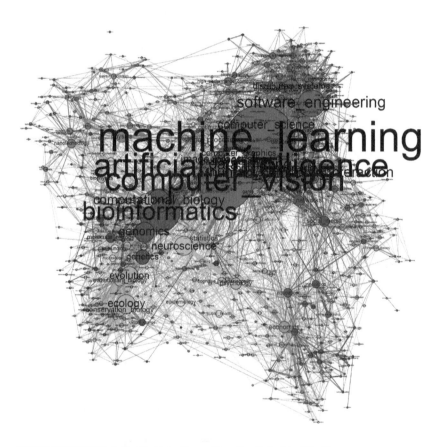

Figure 6.5   **Labels map from Google Scholar Citations (December 2011)**

Source: (Ortega and Aguillo, 2012)

Despite the fact that profiles are created directly by users – which, in theory, should avoid duplicated profiles – 1.35 per cent of repeat profiles were detected, albeit a proportion lower than that of other services. This is possible because an author can create as many profiles as the number of email accounts that he/she has. This also gives rise to the appearance of institutional profiles – of journals, organizations, research groups, and so on – because profile functionalities are adaptable to any research unit (see Figure 6.6). Perhaps the creation of institutional profiles makes up for the absence of aggregated units that group researchers within research areas or organizations – as in the case of Microsoft Academic Search – and enhance this service not only for personal assessments but for organizational and country benchmarking. Although it might be better if these aggregated profiles were included and retrieved in a separate section.

Overall, Google Scholar Citations is an interesting service that enables the user to build a personal homepage from Google Scholar data and build a personal profile that reflects his/her research performance and can be compared with other colleagues through thematic rankings.

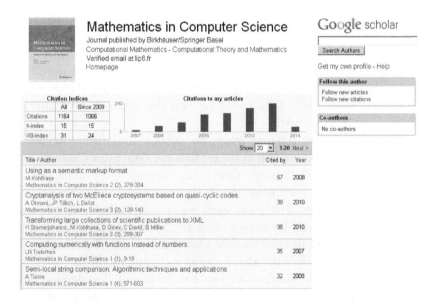

Figure 6.6   Profile of a research journal in Google Scholar Citations

Note: Google and the Google logo are registered trademarks of Google Inc., used with permission

Unlike other profiling services, these profiles are created directly by the user, who has full freedom to include precise information on his/her interests, current place of work and the specific publications authored by him/her and not by other authors with similar names. This should make these profiles more reliable because they could be considered almost as a personal curriculum vitae, although normalized and structured by a unique data model. However, this same freedom could also be to the detriment of the service because of the potential to create false profiles, or to inflate profiles with other authors' papers, or to upload false papers filled with citations to a profile's own papers (Delgado Lopez-Cozar et al., 2012). Perhaps Google needs to develop mechanisms to control these unethical behaviours, although their incidence is only occasional.

Another element of this profiling freedom is that the colonization of the service depends of the willingness of the authors to build a profile – a willingness that is influenced by multiple factors such as accessibility and skill in using web platforms, the desire to make public his/her research activity, or the extent to which a user is in touch with these developments. This can lead to biases in terms of the distribution of the population and, as was seen above, can result in the assignment of profiles being biased towards certain countries, institutions or thematic areas – especially if the service has a particular presence in certain communities. Thus, it could be assumed that the population of Google Scholar Citations is shaped by researchers close to information technologies and social networking environments, and with a particular presence of Brazilian people. For this reason, demographic studies using this population must be considered carefully, taking into account this dynamic environment (Ortega and Aguillo, 2013).

One thing that is missing from this service, and from the other academic search engines, is that the profiles are rather static and do not allow for interaction between them – as happens with online social networking services such as ResearchGate or Academia.edu. The option to 'follow this author' is a good start, but undoubtedly is limited. The service could definitely be improved by adding social networking tools such as forums and internal mailing that would enable the creation of research communities to share opinions and establish working relationships. Google Scholar Citations has the potential to develop as a social networking environment, successfully managing concepts such as Science 2.0 and stressing the development of altmetrics initiatives. In this way, Google Scholar Citations would then compete with both social networking sites and bibliographic indexes.

Google Scholar Metrics

The most recent application that Google added to Google Scholar was Google Scholar Metrics, in April 2012 (Google Scholar Blog, 2012). It claims to be a useful resource to help the location of relevant academic journals in a speciality or country, displaying different rankings of journals according to in-house and standardized bibliometric indicators. Unlike the rest of Google Scholar's services, Google Scholar Metrics is a static source. This means that the bibliometric indicators and the list of papers in each journal are not automatically updated when the citations are computed, as occurs generally within Google Scholar. The updating frequency is roughly annual, with the last two upgrades taking place in November 2012 and July 2013, which suggests a rather low degree of currency. Another important limitation is that the service only includes journals that have published more than 100 articles in the last five years – this being a significant restriction to bibliometric analyses. Perhaps the biggest problem is that the service is not connected to the main Google Scholar database, so it is not possible to locate journals in Google Scholar Metrics and then access their articles in Google Scholar – which raises the question of what is the actual value of this application.

Access to the service is made directly from the main page of Google Scholar, connecting with the main ranking, the top 100 English-language journals – the most representative scientific journals from around the world that publish articles written in English. This ranking is sorted by the h5-index and the h5-median as secondary criteria.

Similar rankings can be observed for other relevant languages in the scientific publishing world (Chinese, Portuguese, German, Spanish, French, Italian, Japanese and Dutch). In each ranking, Google Scholar Metrics lists the top 100 journal titles with the highest h5-index (though only in the case of the English language does Google Scholar Metrics present a subject matter classification scheme that groups the journals by a thematic criterion). This classification framework is structured across two hierarchical levels and has been developed by Google itself. In addition, some subcategories are shared with distinct main categories – for example, 'Economic History' is included in 'Social Sciences' and 'Business, Economics & Management' and incorporates the same journals. A very short list of 20 journals is presented for each research category and subcategory. Clicking in the h5-index value for each journal, it is possible to see the journal's position in several rankings if it is included in the top 100 titles. In addition, the application allows the user to view the list of papers that have contributed to the journal's h-index. Thus, if the journal has an h5-index=23, only those 23 records are presented, in a list sorted by the number of citations.

All this means that it is rather hard to know exactly how many journals are indexed in Google Scholar Metrics. An approximation was calculated by searching for the list of Microsoft Academic Search's journals in Google Scholar Metrics. It was anticipated that this procedure would also enable a comparison of the coverage of Google Scholar Metrics to that of Microsoft Academic Search. The results show that 16,911 unique titles were found, and based on the number of repeat titles it is possible to estimate almost 30,000 journal titles using the capture–re-capture formula (Ortega and Aguillo, 2012).

The list of journal titles is taken from several publisher platforms, but with no cleaning or homogenization process which points to a hasty and rather careless procedure. This results in the existence of duplicated journals with slight variations in the title, such as *Beiträge zur Geschichte der deutschen Sprache und Literatur*, *Bunseki Kagaku* or *Atención primaria*, or of journals that have changed name appearing as separate journals, as with the *Journal of the American Society for Information Science and Technology* and its former title, the *Journal of the American Society for Information Science*.

Evaluating this list of journals, it is interesting to note the inclusion of several sources that strictly speaking should not be considered to be scientific journals (Delgado López-Cózar and Cabezas-Clavijo, 2012a). So, for example, it includes: the different thematic sections of arXiv.org, a thematic repository of pre-prints; several technical series such as *USDA Forest Service General Technical Reports PNW* or working papers such as *Working Paper Series in Economics and Institutions of Innovation* from CESIS at the Royal Institute of Technology; and certain books' series that are considered as research journals, such as the *Springer Series in Materials Science*, including books chapters as articles. The listing also contained journals that do not publish research articles at all, such as *Air Force Magazine* or *American Fitness*, the inclusion of which is surprising not only in Google Scholar Metrics but also in Google Scholar. The inclusion of material such as this is contentious because it does not pass a peer-review process and the quality of its content may be questionable. Moreover, it is possible that many of these e-prints or working papers would be published later in journals, meaning that the contribution might be counted twice, once in each venue. On the other hand, however, the inclusion of such sources extends the scope of the research activity and the reach of these publications, even though they have not been published officially, because there are papers in these venues which are not published in journals but which, however, do have an impact on the scientific community. Furthermore, and as with other search engines, conference proceedings are also included in the mix.

Google Scholar uses two in-house adaptations of the h-index to rank these journals because it is appropriate for aggregated research units such as journals, organizations or countries, in addition to it not being a proprietary algorithm such as the impact factor (Thomson ISI) or SNIP (Scopus). The h5-index counts the number of papers (h) from a journal that have received equal or more citations than h. This is calculated only with articles published in the previous five years as a way to capture only the most recent impact. The h5-median is an internal proposal that calculates the median of citations from the same articles included in the h5-index. However, these indicators favour research units with an extensive career, with a bias towards journals that publish more articles than others. The h5-median is an unusual measurement, the value and usefulness of which is not clear because it does not offer anything more than is provided by the h5-index – raising the question of whether it is a mere artefact to help rank journals with a similar h5-index. Furthermore, the median of citations used in the h5-index was calculated for some journals and the results did not correspond to the figures presented in Google Scholar Metrics, so the true calculation of this index is unknown.

In summary, the first impressions of this tool reveal not only its too-hasty development but its naïve approach to bibliometrics and to the research journal evaluation. Ranging from the indicators used to the language classification criteria, there are clear signs of ignorance on how to evaluate a research journal and how to know which data structure should contribute more precise information on the quality or performance of a journal. Indeed, it is difficult to comprehend the real purpose of Google Scholar Metrics and what Google Scholar expects to offer with the service because there is no 'about us' section or help page to explain its intention. Thus, for example, the use of the h-index is an acceptable criterion with which to rank journals, but it is unacceptable and meaningless to present only the papers that contribute to the h-index of the journal. From the perspective of a search engine user, the most important aspect is to work with an interface that retrieves articles by venues, a feature not yet possible in Google Scholar. If Google Scholar Metrics displays only a fraction of the articles from a journal, then the real point of this service is not known. This is even more evident when the information is already accessible through Google Scholar, and Google Scholar Metrics should be a natural gateway to the exploration of Google Scholar from the venue view.

Another controversial decision that betrays the Google developers' lack of knowledge of bibliometrics is that the journals are grouped by language – a unique and extraordinary decision. In order to obtain a reliable assessment of the potential of a journal it should be observed in a disciplinary context because citation patterns between disciplines are so different that ranking medical and history journals together does not offer any qualitative information, being simply a senseless initiative. Moreover, and absurdly, if the English-language journals are indeed classified within subject categories, why can't the rest of the journals also be aggregated to those categories. However, and contrary to the views of Delgado López-Cózar and Robinson-García (2012b), the inclusion of repositories, book series and working paper series would be an interesting idea because it would enable an approximation of the scientific impact of this type of material, which usually is not considered within other research indexes and in other journal evaluation processes. Nevertheless, these sources should only include papers that have not been published subsequently in research journals because the obtained figures would not be comparable.

Overall, it would appear that Google Scholar Metrics was a rushed development with many flaws and developed from a deep ignorance of research journal evaluation and bibliometric indicators (Jacsó, 2012). Addressing these failures and errors – mainly in the definition of the role of the service itself – would enhance this service hugely and would make it a good example of the assessment of international publication venues. Currently, however, this service is merely a distraction for playing with journal rankings and finding a venue's most-cited papers (Delgado López-Cózar and Cabezas-Clavijo, 2012a).

The most exhaustive academic search engine

The sudden rise of Google Scholar on the academic scene was a milestone for academic search engines because it introduced a new perspective on scientific literature and of its impact. Improving on the autonomous citation indexing philosophy of CiteSeer and running the strong harvesting capacities of its bots, Google Scholar became the largest scientific database, regularly updated and open to everyone on the web. Google Scholar broke with the distinct ruling paradigms of scientific bibliographic information. Firstly, it made scientific information freely available to everyone, popularizing science and helping researchers with certain resources to gain access to publication data, which enhanced the research performance of developing countries. Secondly, it covered not only peer-reviewed journals but all types of academic material hosted on the web, from books, technical reports and patents to presentations, pre-prints and conference proceedings. This expanded the concept of research activity to other important products that previously were excluded from the main citation databases, unaware of the impact and importance of these items for the academic community. This is evident within disciplines with a high rate of obsolescence, such as computer science, which relied on conference communications, the impact and value of which were never considered before (Harzing and Van der Wal, 2007). This in turn widened the citing possibility of research articles to compute citations from a broad range of materials, which indicates the importance of these materials in a general academic framework not exclusively related to the scientific research environment (Meho and Yang, 2006). So, for example, this policy allowed the user to study the impact of certain papers in books (Kousha and Thelwall, 2009) or online presentations (Thelwall and Kousha, 2008) which highlights the importance of some works for non-strictly research activities such as teaching or science popularization.

Perhaps one of the most important drawbacks of this citation policy of Google Scholar's is that such materials have not passed a peer-review process, thus the quality and accuracy of the citing contributions have not been verified by the scientific community (Delgado López-Cózar, and Cabezas-Clavijo, 2012a). But then this line of thinking is based on the traditional predominance of the venue as the guarantor of an article's quality. It is my opinion that the citations themselves are the element that guarantees the quality of research, independent of the publication source. Thus, citations from pre-prints or presentations should not be considered of poorer quality; rather, they highlight an influence other than peer-reviewed journals as important. What is disturbing, however, are the possibilities of citation manipulation and spam practices that might be generated by an uncontrolled system (Beel and Gipp, 2010; Delgado López-Cozar et al., 2012). Google Scholar's citation policy contained important gaps that could facilitate the deliberate manipulation of profiles in order to artificially enhance the performance of researchers. For example, Google Scholar can index false documents uploaded to repositories, authored by a fake author and full of citations to that author at a particular institution, resulting in bibliometric indicators for certain people or institutions that have been deliberately falsified.

This forces Google Scholar to adopt stricter controls on these documents in order to detect possible 'citation farms'; not to do so would completely invalidate the service's utility as an evaluation tool for the research community.

Google Scholar suffers from the standard problems common to autonomous citation indexes such as data parsing errors, incorrectly assigned citations and duplicated documents. These were its Achilles heel for a long time and were the subject of several key critiques (Jacsó, 2005a, 2005b; Bar-Ilan, 2008). Fortunately, Google Scholar is making a big effort to resolve these limitations and has increased its consistency and reliability – an indication of the importance the service attaches to the quality of its data integration. However, the citation count is an ongoing matter that Google Scholar has to address with the utmost diligence because its reputation as a research evaluation tool rests absolutely on this issue.

Perhaps one of the most problematic issues for Google Scholar is the absolute absence of information on the running of the service, its coverage and the significance of its results (Gray et al., 2012). This is a general Google policy but is counter-productive for specialized search engines for which these elements are key to gaining the confidence of their users. Instead of a help page, Google Scholar employs a frequently asked questions (FAQ) system, which in fact is oriented more towards informing users how they must utilize the service and adopt the Google sites in order to be successfully crawled by Googlebot than a genuine help page that explains how much data it contains, what its principal sources are, how the documents are indexed, and which shortcuts can be used. At times Google Scholar displays an arrogance towards the user, adopting a patronizing tone while leading users to explore the service in the way it would like them to, and not according to the users' needs. For example, Google Scholar's developers argue that the system only shows up to 1000 results because 'the purpose of the result count is to help users refine their queries and not coverage checking' (Google Scholar, 2014a). This statement is just one example of Google Scholar's lack of interest in satisfying the users' needs and in being transparent about its data and functioning. This opacity becomes more problematic alongside the engine's crucial inconsistencies and limitations of its search system – such as the rounding-up of results, the limit of 1000 records and the incoherent figures displayed when button checks or Booleans operators are used. It is thus not surprising that the principal doubts about its legitimacy as a research evaluation tool spring from the poor quality of information about its coverage (Bauer and Bakkalbasi, 2005; Noruzi,

2005; Northwestern University Library, 2014) and citation counts (Jacsó, 2005b). The most disturbing aspect is that this approach continues – as evidenced in the scaling-down of the advanced search in the most recent make-over in May 2012, in which the search-by-subject option was removed. This further complicates the retrieval of information that demonstrates the coverage of the engine, while raising more doubts about how the system functions.

Yet another drawback of Google Scholar is the poor integration of its added services – Google Scholar Citations and Google Scholar Metrics – into its general structure. Both seem more like half measures developed from the urgency to keep pace with competitor developments than genuine extensions of Google Scholar's capabilities to enhance the search expectations of users and enrich the information contained in its databases. In addition to requiring further development – especially Google Scholar Metrics – both need to unify their search interfaces to search profiles, documents and venues independently, and to allow information to cross over horizontally between different entities – enabling a better appreciation of the information available through Google Scholar and moving it closer to the Microsoft Academic Search model. For example, if the journals in Google Scholar Metrics are classified by subject, why not extend this classification to Google Scholar and make it possible to retrieve documents by journal subject classifications? Or, if Google Scholar Citations can identify each profile's publications, why does it not permit the user to filter a search by profiles? The implementation of all these changes would result in a more robust and compact search engine in which all sections are connected with the entire service, helping it to become a trustworthy research evaluation and benchmarking instrument.

7

Other academic search engines

Abstract: This chapter examines other important academic search engines which due to their functionality and sources do not have their own chapter. First, we look at BASE – a search engine specialized in open sources and built on open protocols that allow it to harvest mainly institutional repositories and digital libraries. Next, Q-Sensei Scholar is examined because it is a promising filtering tool, although based on only five sources. Finally, WorldWideScience is studied as an example of a federated search engine fuelled by bibliographic databases from scientific agencies all over the world; this model, however, produces a large amount of duplicated results and is very time consuming.

Key words: BASE, Q-Sensei Scholar, WorldWideScience, federated search, filtering search, open access.

In addition to the major academic search engines studied in the previous chapters, there are other minor developments that illustrate new and different approaches to scientific information. For example, BASE embodies a commitment to the open access movement for which it has created a search engine oriented to open materials. Q-Sensei Scholar, on the other hand, is a private product more focused on making available a new indexing and search methodology than on displaying a balanced and exhaustive coverage of scientific data. Finally, WorldWideScience is an example of the capabilities and limitations of a federated model in integrating information from multiple sources and confronting the inscrutable 'deep web'.

BASE

Bielefeld Academic Search Engine (BASE) (*http://www.base-search.net*) is a project of the Bielefeld University Library (Germany) that began in September 2004 with the aim of gathering all the scholarly documents provided by open access repositories (Bielefeld University Library, 2014). BASE collects documents from repositories and digital libraries that follow the Open Archives Initiative Protocol for Metadata Harvesting (OAI-PMH). Thus, 75 per cent of their records are open access, comprising 58.8 million documents from more than 2700 sources. This large variety of sources means that many documents are not described properly by the primary sources.

Founded on digital libraries

Depending on the document type, BASE enables the retrieval of a large variety of materials, including attractive products such as audio, video or software, that are very difficult to locate in other academic engines. However, only 45 per cent of the documents present an identifiable document typology, a consequence of the multiple forms and languages used to specify this kind of metadata. In addition, the assignation of document types by the provider is not always correct and materials such as photographs or maps are sometimes labelled as books or articles. Taking this into account, the most frequent materials are journal articles (47.5 per cent), followed by images (18.7 per cent) and doctoral dissertations (10.4 per cent) (Table 7.1).

BASE also displays the list of its 2700 sources – including repositories, publishers, digital libraries and bibliographic services – and the number of records that contribute to the search engine. Thanks to the OAI-PMH, this enormous amount of heterogeneous sources can be integrated into the same search engine. Table 7.2 highlights the ten most important sources, including the search engine and digital library CiteSeer[x] (5.7 per cent), the thematic repository PubMed Central (5.1 per cent) and the German bibliographic service DataCite Metadata Store (4.06 per cent).

Comprehensive search utilities

Within BASE, only metadata are indexed so the system simply retrieves information contained in those fields. Two search functions are provided: basic and advanced. The basic search admits the use of Boolean

Table 7.1   Distribution of materials by document type in BASE

Document type	Documents	Distribution (%)
Articles	12,534,113	47.55
Images	4,947,860	18.77
Theses	2,740,847	10.40
Reports	2,524,529	9.58
Books	1,936,496	7.35
Primary data	1,137,098	4.31
Maps	203,976	0.77
Book reviews	96,611	0.37
Audio	91,804	0.35
Sheet music	76,378	0.29
Video	63,410	0.24
Software	6,971	0.03
Total	26,360,093	100.00

Table 7.2   The ten most important sources in BASE

Source	Type	Documents	Percentage
CiteSeer[x]	Search engine	3,352,893	5.70
PubMed Central	Thematic repository	3,008,771	5.12
DataCite Metadata Store	Bibliographic service	2,386,194	4.06
HighWire Press	Publisher	2,342,511	3.98
University of Michigan: DLPS	Institutional repository	2,326,339	3.96
Gallica	Institutional repository	2,111,771	3.59
Directory of Open Access Journals	Journal directory	1,573,847	2.68
RePEc	Thematic repository	1,114,209	1.89
Hathi Trust Digital Library	Institutional repository	953,392	1.62
arXiv.org	Thematic repository	912,133	1.55
All sources		58,807,232	100.00

operators, quotations marks and wildcards. BASE also has semantic tools to expand and improve the simple search. Thus, 'Additional word forms' searches for plural, genitive and other forms, while 'Multilingual synonyms' ('EuroVoc Thesaurus') connects the query terms with the EuroVoc thesaurus, a multilingual thesaurus from the European Union, to retrieve synonyms and translations as well. The advanced search enables a structured search by title, author, subject headings and URLs. These delimitations can be directly applied with shortcuts: `tit:` (title), `aut:` (author), `subj:` (subject heading), `url:` (URL) and `pub:` (publisher). In addition, it is also possible to filter the results by content sources, year of publication and document type.

The BASE results page displays ten records by default, although this can be increased to up to 100 (Figure 7.1). Each record contains metadata describing the item, with a direct link to the resource and the content provider. In addition, each record provides a link to Google Scholar to widen the search, and allows the user to export to a large variety of formats and reference manager tools. Looking at the results themselves, BASE reveals a lack of duplicate control because many documents can be deposited in several sources, which means that potentially BASE indexes the same document two or three times.

It is also possible to browse records by document type and subject matter. BASE uses the Dewey Decimal Classification (DDC) system to arrange the documents. The classification assignation is performed in two ways: some documents are already classified by the providers and

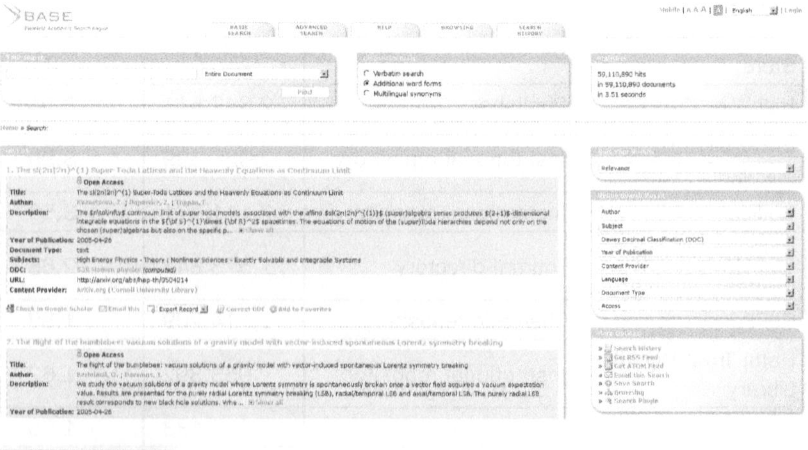

Figure 7.1   BASE results page (11 March 2014)

the remainder are classified using an automatic classification process (Lösch et al., 2011). However, the classification programme is not complete and only 16.4 per cent of the records have been assigned to a research area. Thus, the most predominant disciplines are science (30 per cent), technology (27.3 per cent) and the social sciences (18.1 per cent) (see Table 7.3). With the exception of computer science (8.27 per cent), the remaining disciplines fall within the humanities which – combined with arts and recreation – represent 16.3 per cent, a considerable proportion compared to other academic search engines.

An engine for open access

As indicated above, BASE is an academic search engine the main purpose of which is to provide a gateway to the scientific literature freely available on the web. It started out as a support tool for the open access movement, gathering and disseminating academic results housed in open repositories and digital libraries. Technically, it is based on the power of the OAI-PMH protocol to integrate metadata from a huge variety of sources and hence build a large search engine (58.8 million documents), the main attraction of which is that more than 75 per cent of its records point to free documents. Unlike other commercial search engines, BASE is completely transparent about its functioning and coverage. Perhaps

Table 7.3 Distribution of documents in BASE according to the Dewey Decimal Classification system

Research area	Documents	Distribution (%)
Science	2,882,240	30.01
Technology	2,623,047	27.31
Social Sciences	1,737,974	18.10
Arts & Recreation	484,687	5.05
Computer Science	794,479	8.27
History & Geography	419,488	4.37
Philosophy & Psychology	289,488	3.01
Language	217,279	2.26
Religion	105,570	1.10
Literature	49,656	0.52
Total	9,603,908	100.00

imbued by the spirit of open access this product makes it easy to explore its entire database via statistics and a good search interface, allowing a complete examination of its contents and working. Nevertheless, simply by extracting the data from multiple sources and indexing the metadata directly reduces the reliability of the results because of the inconsistency of the primary sources. So, for example, with regard to the document type definition, the absence of subject matter classifications and the presence of multiple duplicate records suggests that a data warehousing process is required to normalize and homogenize the data.

Another potential problem is that not all the documents uploaded to a repository are the result of a research process, and many of them have not passed a control process. For example, Gallica is a comprehensive repository of the Bibliothèque nationale de France (BnF) which includes historic digitalized documents, and the Hathi Trust Digital Library has a high proportion of educative materials. The large proportion of items from the humanities as well as the significant presence of images, reports and books reinforce this argument. Yet, despite these minor problems of data robustness and some doubt over BASE's scientific coverage, this search engine is without doubt the principal gateway to open access documents due to its comprehensiveness and huge coverage of sources – enhanced by a transparent policy and a friendly interface.

Q-Sensei Scholar

Q-Sensei Scholar (*http://scholar.qsensei.com*) is an academic search engine specializing in search solutions which was created by the company Q-Sensei and which originated from the fusion of Lalisio (Germany) and QUASM Inc. (United States) in 2007. Q-Sensei Scholar was born in 2008 and is a free web-based service which gives access to more than 40 million books and scholarly articles from five selected sources (Quint, 2008; Q-Sensei Scholar, 2014). It takes a multidimensional approach in which any search result can be filtered by multiple attributes, making it possible to minimize or expand the query as well as navigate across the different dimensions in which retrieved documents can be arranged. So, for example, the results page not only displays the resulting records but also presents a top menu that groups those documents according to up to eight characteristics, namely: document type, key word, publication year, author, journal, publisher, language and source. These groups are clickable and act as navigational tools that delimit the query, selecting the desirable results according to the informational need.

A limited range of sources

This multidimensional data structure makes it enormously easy to explore the content of the search engine and describe its coverage.

Table 7.4 describes the distribution of contents based on the five sources that feed Q-Sensei Scholar, highlighting MEDLINE/PubMed (51.9 per cent), followed by the Library of Congress (28 per cent) and the web publishing platform ingentaconnect (14.4 per cent). This small range of sources could impact on the thematic and typological distribution of the indexed documents because other important research sources that could contribute with different documents are left out. So, for example, 99.8 per cent of the books come from the Library of Congress, the only document type that this source contributes. Looking at the research articles, only ingentaconnect could be considered a multidisciplinary source, while MEDLINE specializes in medicine, RePEc specializes in economics and arXiv.org specializes in physics. Thus, important disciplines such as chemistry, biology, engineering or the humanities could be under-represented. This would be very obvious if a subject matter classification system was in operation.

One other important point is that if arXiv.org and RePEc were counted as open repositories, only 5.5 per cent of Q-Sensei Scholar records would link to free contents. MEDLINE/PubMed may also include open access materials, but, focusing on the publishers within this source, only the Public Library of Science (PLOS) and Hindawi contain open articles and these account for just 0.035 per cent.

Observing the distribution of the main document types in Table 7.5, the most common types of records are research articles (62.8 per cent) and books (25.7 per cent), with reviews trailing far behind (4.2 per cent).

Table 7.4 Distribution of documents by source in Q-Sensei Scholar

Sources	Documents	Distribution (%)
MEDLINE/PubMed	23,140,449	51.98
Library of Congress	12,466,462	28.00
ingentaconnect.com	6,416,965	14.41
RePEc	1,579,436	3.55
arXiv.org	916,293	2.06
Total	44,519,605	100.00

Table 7.5 Distribution of publications by document type in Q-Sensei Scholar

Document type	Documents	Distribution (%)
Research article	30,496,539	62.78
Book	12,484,487	25.70
Review	2,039,908	4.20
Study	1,916,812	3.95
Case report	1,642,709	3.38
Total	48,580,455	100.00

There are also some confusing document types that perhaps correspond to other categories of document. For example, browsing the 'Review' category, these are types of research articles that should be included within 'Research Articles'. The same is true within the 'Study' category – the documents come exclusively from MEDLINE/PubMed and they are in fact research articles. Taking this into account, the proportion of research articles could be greater than 70 per cent.

The strength of filtering

Q-Sensei Scholar could be considered to be more of a directory than a search engine because although it incorporates a search interface that enables document retrieval its key strength is the way in which the contents are structured and can be explored through the multidimensional menu at the top (Figure 7.2). Instead of an advanced search, Q-Sensei Scholar unfolds several filters that delimit and further define the query until the required information is found. The most interesting aspect of this system is that it enables navigation from the broadest piece of information to the most specific data. With a focus on searching, Q-Sensei Scholar indexes and retrieves the complete parts of the record such as the title, author, publication date, venue, key words and abstract. In addition, in the right-hand margin it suggests ways of making the query more precise, such as related key words or papers authored by the same author. However, and as discussed above, its search system is rather simple and the 'exact match' approach it adopts is restrictive. For example, it does not support searching by specific fields nor the use of wildcards and Booleans operators and, further, it is sensitive to accent marks.

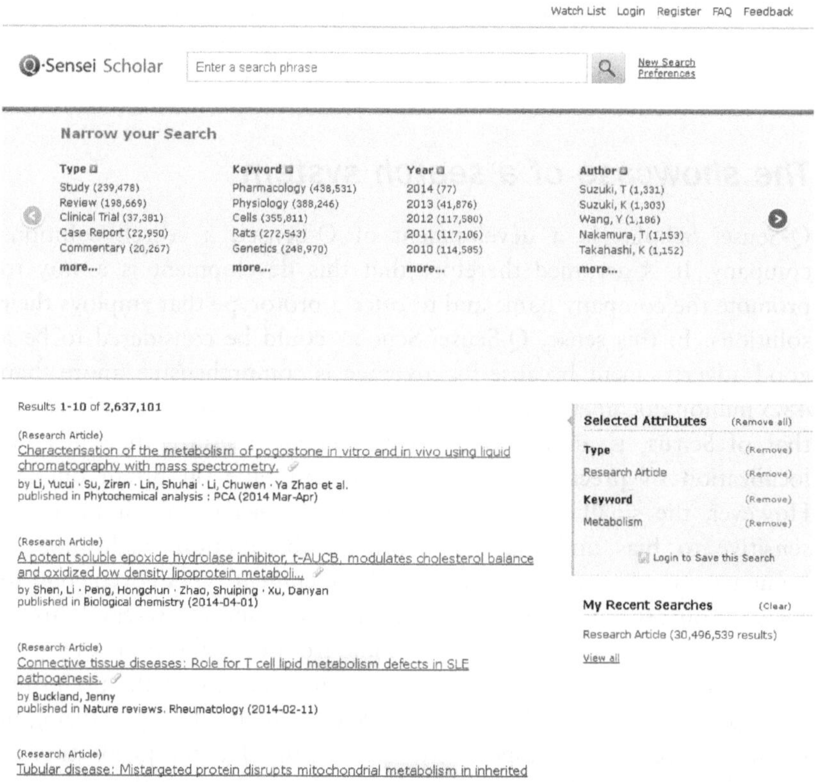

Watch List   Login   Register   FAQ   Feedback

Q·Sensei Scholar

Enter a search phrase

New Search
Preferences

Narrow your Search

Type ▢	Keyword ▢	Year ▢	Author ▢
Study (239,478)	Pharmacology (438,531)	2014 (77)	Suzuki, T (1,331)
Review (198,669)	Physiology (388,246)	2013 (41,876)	Suzuki, K (1,303)
Clinical Trial (37,381)	Cells (355,811)	2012 (117,580)	Wang, Y (1,196)
Case Report (22,950)	Rats (272,543)	2011 (117,106)	Nakamura, T (1,153)
Commentary (20,267)	Genetics (248,970)	2010 (114,595)	Takahashi, K (1,152)
more...	more...	more...	more...

Results 1-10 of 2,637,101

(Research Article)
Characterisation of the metabolism of pogostone in vitro and in vivo using liquid chromatography with mass spectrometry.
by Li, Yucui · Su, Ziran · Lin, Shuhai · Li, Chuwen · Ya Zhao et al.
published in Phytochemical analysis : PCA (2014 Mar-Apr)

(Research Article)
A potent soluble epoxide hydrolase inhibitor, t-AUCB, modulates cholesterol balance and oxidized low density lipoprotein metaboli...
by Shen, Li · Peng, Hongchun · Zhao, Shuiping · Xu, Danyan
published in Biological chemistry (2014-04-01)

(Research Article)
Connective tissue diseases: Role for T cell lipid metabolism defects in SLE pathogenesis.
by Buckland, Jenny
published in Nature reviews. Rheumatology (2014-02-11)

(Research Article)
Tubular disease: Mistargeted protein disrupts mitochondrial metabolism in inherited

Selected Attributes   (Remove all)

Type	(Remove)
Research Article	(Remove)
Keyword	(Remove)
Metabolism	(Remove)

☐ Login to Save this Search

My Recent Searches   (Clear)

Research Article (30,496,539 results)
View all

Figure 7.2   Q-Sensei Scholar results page (11 March 2014)

An openness to users' suggestions

As with other search engines that were analysed, Q-Sensei Scholar enables the correction and modification of records if users perceive mistakes or confusions. Thus, users can log in and edit entries. The engine lists the updates that each user has made and which elements have been modified. It is also possible to suggest a URL that would contain precise and more detailed information about a document. This enhances the service, encouraging users to participate in making the service more reliable as well as to help solve any consistency problems. Modifications can be viewed in 'Latest Changes'. Another point of interest is the 'Search Log', a section which lists the most frequent queries launched to the engine. These are sorted by day and can be viewed by clicking on them. Q-Sensei Scholar is the only search engine that provides this information about its query searches and the results would make interesting material for studying users' searching interests and behaviour.

The showcase of a search system

Q-Sensei Scholar is a development of Q-Sensei, a search solutions company. It is assumed therefore that this development is a way to promote the company name and to offer a prototype that employs their solutions. In this sense, Q-Sensei Scholar could be considered to be a good advertisement because its coverage is comprehensive (more than 48.5 million documents) and its multidimensional system, very similar to that of Scirus, is an easy and usable search interface that aids the localization of precise information and can take on broad queries. However, the small number of data sources means that it might be sensitive to bias and that its document distribution might not be homogeneous. It is possible that certain document types correspond to specific sources which in turn are specialists in specific research areas. So, for example, most of the books come from the Library of Congress and are related to the humanities, while the majority of the pre-prints and open access materials are from arXiv.org or RePEc, specializing in physis and economics respectively. This means that the proportion of research articles on the arts and humanities is minimal, in the same way that the inclusion of books on physics or chemistry is very rare. Apart from this dependence on content sources, the Q-Sensei Scholar architecture is robust, user-friendly and has the possibility for growth – widening and diversifying its contents as well as introducing subject matter classification.

WorldWideScience

WorldWideScience (*http://worldwidescience.org*) is a project led by the Office of Scientific and Technical Information (OSTI) within the United States Department of Energy (DOE) that expects to be an international gateway to scientific portals and databases. WorldWideScience set up an alliance of 17 national libraries and scientific information offices from all around the world. Among their members are the French Institut de l'information scientifique et technique (INIST), the Institute of Scientific and Technical Information of China (ISTIC) and the Japan Science and Technology Agency (JST). In addition to these organizations, WorldWideScience counts on Microsoft Research for its technical support. In this way, WorldWideScience is presented as a central hub that provides access to the great range of scientific databases produced by its members. The alliance began in 2007 with only 12 international databases, now it contains close to 100 sources.

Federated searching

WorldWideScience is based on a federated search system. With this model, WorldWideScience presents a unique search interface that connects to all the databases of the members that collaborate in the consortium. When a query is launched to WorldWideScience it sends this query to every database retrieving the results, these items are then processed in a central server to be ranked and then the system eliminates duplicate records from different sources. This search service is provided by Deep Web Technologies, creator of Explorit Everywhere, a solution to extract data from databases and integrate the results in the same platform. Explorit Everywhere obtains the data through a screen scraping procedure, that is, it harvests the records from the results page and not directly from the database (Deep Web Technologies, 2013). This means that although the database could contain thousands of results that fit the query, Explorit Everywhere only takes the results displayed on the first page. This procedure avoids the key problem of federated searching: the slow speed of the retrieval. The drawback of this system, however, is that a great deal of information is not presented – less relevant for very precise queries, but noticeable in exhaustive searches.

One of the alleged advantages of this system is that it enables the exploration of the 'deep web' (Warnick, 2010). The concept of the 'deep web', or the 'invisible web', refers to the fact that there is a part of the web that is not crawled by the principal search engines – due mainly to protected pages (i.e., intranets), a lack of indexable formats (i.e., Flash), or unlinked pages. But the largest proportion of the invisible web is comprised of web database contents that can only be reached by a query (Bergman, 2001). The WorldWideScience approach aims to solve this problem by connecting the highest number of databases in the same searchable platform. Despite this, however, this search engine retrieves only a small portion of these databases because it displays only the first few results from each source, meaning that its objective is barely accomplished.

More quantity than quality

As outlined above, WorldWideScience acts as a central gateway to all the scientific databases that each participant in the collaboration makes available on the web. It classifies its sources into four categories:

- *English sources* (59) is the largest group and contains sources with a predominant proportion of English language documents.
- *Multilingual sources* (23) groups databases with languages other than English.
- *Multimedia sources* (6) is an interesting group in which it is possible to locate video or podcasts.
- *Data sources* (13) groups repositories containing publicly accessible scientific data.

In total, WorldWideScience could provide access to up to 400 million documents (Warnick, 2010). However, many of these databases present similar information, and in many cases they comprise different language versions of the same interface. For example, the search page of Refdoc, the scientific database of INIST, is in French and English, but WorldWideScience considers both versions to be different databases. The same is true of Driver and J-STAGE. One can also observe a certain amount of confusion between sources. For example, the Life Science Database Archive from Japan shows different results to its twin English database, while the English Life Science Database cross-search actually points to the Life Science Database Archive. This suggests that the databases used to retrieve the results are not always the same as are shown in the list.

WorldWideScience does not provide the total number of records from its sources, so a neutral testing query ("a") was launched to check the system's coverage. 'Source Status' shows the number of records found – displayed by source. Duplicated sources were removed, as explained above.

Table 7.6 displays the sources with the most results. DNA Data Bank of Japan is the largest source with 60.12 per cent of the results, but this is merely a data repository and cannot be considered a bibliographic database exactly. Thus, Refdoc, the INIST database, is the source with

Table 7.6	The ten most important sources by number of results in WorldWideScience (11 March 2014)

Source name	Country	Results	Totals	Percentage
DNA Data Bank of Japan	Japan	90	182,915,234	60.12
Refdoc	France	50	53,374,442	17.54
GetInfo	Germany	55	23,885,694	7.85
Europe PubMed Central		100	17,139,999	5.63
Science.gov	United States	212	9,307,269	3.06
Life Science Database Cross Search	Japan	91	3,816,486	1.25
International Nuclear Information System (INIS)		30	2,746,401	0.90
io-port.net	Germany	100	1,899,899	0.62
Trove	Australia	20	1,381,402	0.45
European Nucleotide Archive	United Kingdom	105	1,277,002	0.42
All sources		5,918	305,558,324	100.00

the most content (17.54 per cent), followed by GetInfo, from the German National Library of Science and Technology (7.85 per cent), and the European gateway of PubMed Central (5.63 per cent). As indicated above, the Life Science Database Archive shows two different results, perhaps due to the fact that one searches only Japanese documents and the other searches only English papers. The 'Totals' column relates to the total number of records indexed by each source, while the 'Results' column presents the number of records captured by WorldWideScience and displayed in the search engine. As explained above, this approach covers only a very small proportion of the original source results. For example, of more than 53.3 million Refdoc records, WorldWideScience takes only 50 – which is an insignificant proportion. For the other services, the figure depends on the number of records that each service can display on its first page. Bringing together all the sources, WorldWideScience displays only 0.004 per cent of the entire potential of these bibliographic services.

One other point of note is the heterogeneous nature of the sources in terms of typology and discipline. Many of these sources are atomized around very specialized issues, the scope of which is very limited. Thus, there is a Greek repository of Ph.D. theses (the National Archive of PhD Theses), a search engine on waste management (Wastenet), the summaries of a historic journal (Transactions and Proceedings of the Royal Society of New Zealand), and so on. In this way, of the 97 sources that feed WorldWideScience, the top ten sources cover more than 97.4 per cent of the engine's content, meaning that the contribution of the remainder is truly trivial.

WorldWideScience shows a results page rich in information on the retrieved records (Figure 7.3). The page is structured around three tabs which split the results according to papers, multimedia and data. Results can be sorted by rank (relevance), date, title and authors, and can be limited to one specific source. The left-hand menu groups the results by topics, authors, publications, publishers and dates, which provides easy data exploration. It also displays an interactive visual classifier, but with a confusing scheme and rather unusual categories. Finally, the engine connects with Wikipedia and the news service EurekAlert! to provide a definition of the search term and related news about the query terms.

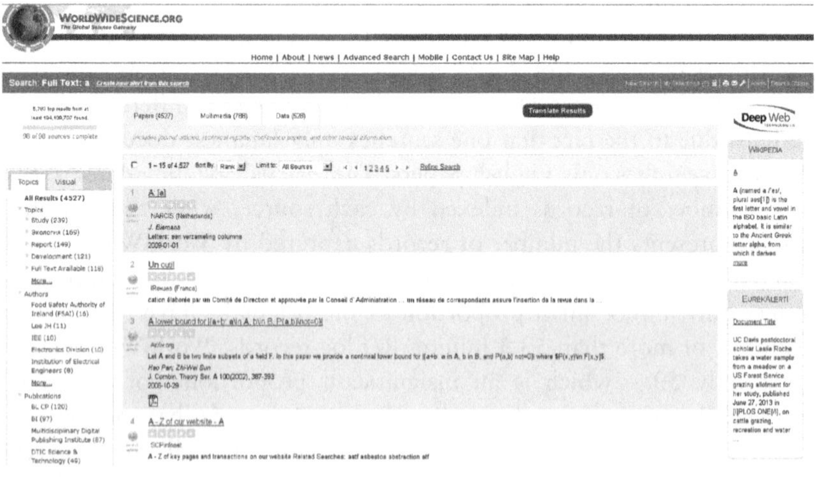

Figure 7.3   WorldWideScience results page (11 March 2014)

The weakness of non-integrated sources

WorldWideScience aims to be a unique portal of access to a large variety of scientific data through a federated searching model. The project is supported by a global consortium of scientific information agencies which are trying to make their databases accessible through an integrated search engine. However, the system is rather limited in terms of its capabilities. The federated model implemented by Deep Web Technologies does not produce the expected results. The screen scraping method does not work well enough because it leaves out a huge amount of information, and it is not a reliable method if the aim is the creation of a federated system. It is surprising that this search engine is endorsed by an international consortium, and yet the technical procedure is limited to scraping the results from only the first page, a task that could be accomplished by a simple crawl. Even more surprising is that the service claims to be a solution to the 'deep web', while actually using such a superficial technique. I suggest that this service should integrate and store the data in the same database, which would increase its speed and achieve a greater degree of consistency facilitating the consortium's entire data rather than only the first few results. I also recommend that the selection of sources should be streamlined – because many of them are rather small and it is possible that their contents are duplicated with others – which would reduce the processing time and increase the engine's reliability.

8

A comparative analysis

Abstract: In this chapter, the search engines analysed in the previous chapters are compared in order to study the common, principal characteristics that an academic search tool has to have. From qualitative aspects such as functioning and exporting to quantitative issues such as coverage, material sources and types of materials, this chapter reviews the advantages and shortcomings of each engine. Thus, Google Scholar is the engine with the broadest coverage, but BASE is the device with the most open access items. Based on profiling services, Microsoft Academic Search is outstanding, while Scirus owns the best search interface and WorldWideScience and CiteSeer[x] operate the best exporting solutions.

Key words: functioning, coverage, open access, exporting, searching.

A comparative analysis of the academic search engines studied in this book will be undertaken in this chapter. The main objective is to analyse these systems from different perspectives, providing a multi-layered view of the performance of each search service. In this way, this comparative approach will highlight the advantages and shortcomings of each search engine in relation to the others, stressing the significance of each aspect. The intention is not that of a competitive process to select the best search engine for scientific information; instead this is a process to contextualize the performance of these search tools in relation to the others as a way to describe their advantages or to highlight their weaknesses.

Functioning

Differences or similarities between search engines are initially marked by the way in which they are set up and the purpose of each service. Many of them were created with a specific intention and focused on specific users or materials. However, the means used to accomplish their objective sometimes are not the most appropriate. For example, essentially two different ways of obtaining data were observed: crawling the web space looking for academic materials; and selecting specific sources that provide bibliographic records (see Table 8.1). Scirus, CiteSeer[x] and Google Scholar adopt the first method – using a bot to compile the information directly from the web, while Microsoft Academic Search, BASE, Q-Sensei Scholar, AMiner and WorldWideScience take their data from secondary sources. A mixed approach is also possible – Scirus uses web pages as well as authoritative sources, and Microsoft Academic Search and AMiner obtain some of their information from web crawling.

Each method of data gathering has its advantages and drawbacks. The use of a web crawler favours a comprehensive coverage of academic objects accessible on the web and the ability to build a searchable database quickly. In this sense, it is noticeable that search engines based on web crawling – such as Scirus and Google Scholar – display a considerable number of records. However, much of this information is not structured and a robust parsing mechanism is necessary to create a consistent and reliable search engine. These types of engines are also more likely to contain important data mistakes; CiteSeer[x] and Google Scholar both contain inconsistencies in identifying titles, authors, dates

Table 8.1 Means of obtaining and accessing data by search engine

Search engine	Data obtaining	Data accesing
Scirus	Crawling, secondary sources	Filtering, searching
WorldWideScience	Secondary sources	Searching (federated system)
Google Scholar	Crawling	Searching
Microsoft Academic Search	Crawling, secondary sources	Directory, searching
BASE	Secondary sources	Searching
Q-Sensei Scholar	Secondary sources	Filtering, searching
AMiner	Secondary sources	Directory, searching
CiteSeer[x]	Crawling	Searching

or venues, although Google Scholar is successfully addressing these problems. The use of secondary sources solves the aforementioned problems because the data are gathered in a structured format and less time and effort is spent processing and harvesting. Microsoft Academic Search, AMiner, BASE, Q-Sensei Scholar and WorldWideScience are good examples of this method.

However, the use of secondary sources does not entirely rule out the previous problem because errors can also exist in secondary sources. It was observed that many of the mistakes in AMiner came straight from BDLP or CiteSeer[x], and that the significant presence of duplicated authors in Microsoft Academic Search is caused by the different ways in which an author is described in the metadata supplied by CrossRef. This issue of duplicated records is perhaps the most serious problem of secondary sources because it is highly likely that the same record will be indexed in multiple sources. In this sense, the best search engine is Google Scholar which groups together all the variations of the same entry – unlike WorldWideScience, Q-Sensei Scholar, BASE and, to a lesser extent, Microsoft Academic Search which all display a considerable number of duplicated records, distorting the actual coverage of the service. Another problem is caused by each source's limitations of coverage, which could affect the general thematic or typological distribution of the search engine. Thus, for example, Q-Sensei Scholar is supported by only five sources, many of them specializing in certain thematic areas and in specific document typologies, which produces an unbalanced service. Another example is Microsoft Academic Search, 90 per cent of whose data come from CrossRef, including only papers from publishers associated with that platform.

Obviously each search engine incorporates mechanisms to enable the retrieval of data through a search query, depending on the form in which the data are accessed by the users. However, in addition to these search interfaces which will be discussed below, there are other ways in which to obtain the data that have specific advantages or shortcomings. With the exception of CiteSeer[x], which only incorporates a search box, all the other engines facilitate additional ways to explore their data (see Table 8.1). The most common method is the filter that delimits and selects the most specific results based on the search needs. This function ranges from Google Scholar's very simple version with year and document type filters to the exhaustive filtering systems of Scirus and Q-Sensei Scholar which allow the user to select any document according to a large variety of characteristics such as publication date, source, document type, key words, and so on. In many instances, these filtering systems aim to compensate for deficiencies in the searching system, such as a poor advanced search or the absence of tips, operators and wildcards as with Q-Sensei Scholar.

Another common method is to arrange data within a directory or ranking that assists data exploration through sorted lists or structured menus – as exemplified by AMiner and Microsoft Academic Search. With regard to the former, its search system is so limited than it needs additional means of presenting its data such as author rankings, topic lists and journals directories. Microsoft Academic Search, on the other hand, adopts the directory shape because its information is structured within several multi-levels that describe distinct aggregated objects, and a directory across several levels enables more efficient navigation and analysis of the information.

WorldWideScience is an example of a search mechanism that is becoming obsolete: the federated search. This type of search acts as a gateway which launches the query to several search engines at the same time, taking each engine's results and displaying them in the results page. Earlier examples of this were metasearch engines such as MetaCrawler or HotBot. Nowadays, this model is used for commercial companies' search services in the areas of travelling (KAYAK) or for comparison engines such as FindTheBest. However, within the academic search environment this type of search system presents several problems such as poor duplicate control and, above all, a lack of speed in processing and obtaining information from different sources.

Structure

One of the features which best describes the aim of these engines and which distinguishes them from traditional citation indexes is the implementation of profiles at different levels (Table 8.2). This aggregated method of data representation extracts valuable information about profiles' research activity, which helps with research decision making and in obtaining a detailed and contextualized picture of scientific production and impact on several levels. Only half of the engines incorporate some kind of profiling device. AMiner was the pioneer in profiling authors, journals and subject classes, although its definition of topics is quite limited, as has been discussed. However, the search engine that implements this feature most effectively is Microsoft Academic Search, the only service that includes organizations and a structured

Table 8.2   Entities profiling by search engine

Search engine	Authors	Journals	Organizations	Subject class
Microsoft Academic Search	Yes	Yes	Yes	Yes
AMiner	Yes	Yes	No	Yes
Google Scholar	Yes	Yes	No	No
CiteSeer[x]	Yes	No	No	No
BASE	No	No	No	No
Scirus	No	No	No	No
WorldWideScience	No	No	No	No
Q-Sensei Scholar	No	No	No	No

classification scheme. On the back of this, Google Scholar has recently added two profiling services for authors (Google Scholar Citations) and journals (Google Scholar Metrics). CiteSeer[x] presents a simple author profile but this only includes papers, addresses and the h-index.

Although there is no significant difference in terms of the information displayed in the profiles, there is a big difference in terms of the way in which the user interacts with his/her own profile. Within AMiner and Microsoft Academic Search profiles are created automatically by the system from the bibliographic records, which increases the likelihood of duplicate profiles due to the different ways in which the same author entitles papers. However, the removal, merging and modification of profiles can be suggested by users of Microsoft Academic Search, and profiles can be edited directly in AMiner. The Google Scholar model, on the other hand, is radically different: profiles are created directly by the user, simply by filling in a web form, and publications can be added, indexed in Google Scholar. This system avoids duplicate profiles and the updating is immediate. However, the drawbacks are that is difficult to normalize affiliations, there is no subject classification system and profiles could easily be altered intentionally.

Coverage

Perhaps the most important elements when evaluating a search engine are the coverage and amount of indexed documents. The more documents that are retrieved, the greater the probability of satisfying the users' needs. This requires a technical and intellectual infrastructure that can supply the information successfully. In fact, this is such an important issue that many search services have publicized their coverage as a sign of their prestige and strength. However, the largest search engines are now removing this information so that their actual coverage, and any deficiencies in it, cannot be easily checked or detected. For this same reason, many search engines do not assist in the calculation of the amount of their content, focusing their search interfaces more on precision rather than on recall. These transparency policies range from the complete opacity of Google Scholar to the open philosophy of BASE. Thus, many of the numbers in this book were obtained from basic procedures such as crawling samples, screen scraping, sequential querying, and so on – which means that they are merely approximations as to the size of these search engines.

Table 8.3 and Figure 8.1 indicate the number of each search engine's retrievable records, based on the information provided by the engine itself in some cases or based on personal estimation in others. The engine that makes the most documents available to the user is Scirus, with 662 million documents. This huge figure is due to the fact that 86 per cent of Scirus' records are academic web pages. A fair comparison would suggest 87.3 million research papers, which still ranks it among the largest search engines. However, it is possible that the number of unique records is lower because, as discussed in Chapter 3, Scirus managed duplicate records badly and counted the same documents included in multiple sources as different documents. This problem is prevalent in

Table 8.3   Search engine coverage (February 2014)

Search engine	Research articles	Other materials	Total
Scirus	87,300,000	574,700,000	662,000,000
WorldWideScience	100,000,000	300,000,000	400,000,000
Google Scholar	64,000,000	45,000,000	109,000,000
Microsoft Academic Search	39,800,000	0	39,800,000
BASE	26,300,000	32,500,000	58,800,000
Q-Sensei Scholar	30,500,000	18,100,000	48,600,000
AMiner	2,500,000	0	2,500,000
CiteSeer[x]	3,300,000	0	3,300,000

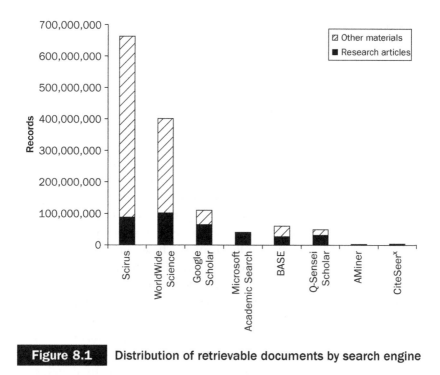

Figure 8.1 Distribution of retrievable documents by search engine

search engines that do not harvest or integrate the information themselves but use secondary sources to feed their results with no duplication control. The same is true of WorldWideScience with 400 million documents; in fact, this is a gateway to more than 90 sources which provide those 400 million documents. In addition to the fact that it is also not able to remove duplicate records from multiple sources, WorldWideScience displays only the first few results for each secondary source – meaning that the supposed 400 million documents in fact is turned into a hundred thousand documents, or less (Warnick, 2010).

The third-ranked source in terms of number of retrievable records is Google Scholar (109 million documents) which, deducting court opinions and patents, suggests a figure of more than 64 million research documents. Microsoft Academic Search presents 39.8 million documents (Microsoft, 2014), all of which are research articles published in peer-reviewed journals. BASE, the open access engine, shows similar figures but includes other types of research materials, of which only 26.3 million would correspond to research articles. Q-Sensei Scholar shows a little fewer, with 48.6 million documents, of which 30.5 million can be considered to be research articles. As per Scirus and WorldWideScience, Q-Sensei Scholar also obtains its data from secondary sources with no duplicate control and therefore it is possible that the actual number of research articles would fall short of the suggested 30.5 million.

Far below these sources are CiteSeer[x], with only 3.3 million research publications obtained from crawling the web, and AMiner, with 2.5 million research papers and conference proceedings mostly sourced from DBLP. It should be pointed out that these last two search engines focus mainly on computer science, which explains their small size.

One important aspect of coverage is the number and proportion of full-text scientific documents that can be made available by the search engines. The fact that most of the web is public and that the open access movement demands full access to the results of research has influenced the search engines in their fulfilment of the function of retrieving and locating this material available on the web. This means that the degree of access to these documents could be an interesting qualitative indicator of the ability of these engines to provide the items demanded by the research community – and of their interest in doing so (Table 8.4 and Figure 8.2). In this way, BASE, the search engine specializing in open access materials, is the service that offers the most full-text documents, with approximately 44 million – 75 per cent of the total indexed. WorldWideScience can give access to approximately 31 million full-text documents from repositories and digital libraries (although many of these documents could be duplicates); even so, this is only 0.7 per cent of the documents available through this engine. In third place, Google Scholar brings together almost 13.8 million documents, of which in the region of 28 per cent are open articles, excluding citations, patents and

Table 8.4 Number of full-text documents and their percentage by search engine

Search engine	Articles	Percentage
BASE	44,000,000	75.0
WorldWideScience	31,000,000	0.7
Google Scholar	13,783,900	28.0
CiteSeer[x]	3,300,000	100.0
Scirus	2,799,000	5.6
Q-Sensei Scholar	2,500,000	5.6
Microsoft Academic Search	768,000	5.2

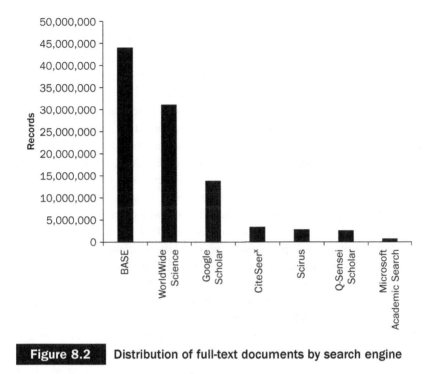

Figure 8.2 Distribution of full-text documents by search engine

court opinions. CiteSeer[x] is the only source that indexes freely available papers on the web exclusively, with 3.3 million. In fifth and sixth places, Scirus and Q-Sensei Scholar show very similar figures and percentages, with 2.8 million articles (5.61 per cent) for Scirus and 2.5 million articles (5.60 per cent) for Q-Sensei Scholar. Finally, Microsoft Academic Search is the engine with the least number of full-text documents, with 0.7 million (5.2 per cent). It is possible that this figure could be higher because this engine also acts as a digital library uploading research papers, but this proportion is not known.

One aspect to take into account when evaluating a search engine is the thematic distribution of its documents, which will indicate the subject matter classification system, the way in which a subject is defined and assigned, and any unbalanced clusters. The thematic distribution of documents gives an insight into the search engine's proportionate coverage of a particular discipline and can determine if that particular engine is the most appropriate tool for a specific research area. However, this is a difficult comparison to make because classification schemes are very different between engines, and some search engines may not even have one. In this context, only Scirus, Microsoft Academic Search and BASE have a structured classification system which would allow such comparisons. The Scirus and BASE systems were adapted to the Microsoft Academic Search system to better fit the disciplinary coverage. Table 8.5 and Figure 8.3 highlight how the distribution in all three cases follows a very different pattern. For example, Microsoft Academic Search displays a balanced coverage in which classical disciplines such as medicine (23.5 per cent of papers), physics (9.8 per cent of papers) and chemistry (8.6 per cent of papers) prevail. Scirus, on the other hand, better represents biological disciplines such as medicine (27.7 per cent), biology (16.9 per cent) and agricultural science (10.4 per cent). Finally, BASE displays a radically different distribution in which the social sciences and humanities are best represented. Thus, the social sciences (18.1 per cent) and the arts and humanities (16.3 per cent) are the largest classes, followed by medicine (13.09 per cent) and economics and business (7.7 per cent).

Microsoft Academic Search, Scirus and BASE are three good examples that emphasize the importance of maintaining a good classification system, and how sensible this is for the sources that feed the system. The above confirms that not all the search engines perform as well on subject matter queries, and it is vital that the user understands the subject class distribution to assess the adequacy of each engine for their needs. It is unfortunate that important search tools such as Google Scholar and AMiner do not have a classification system because this an essential element for academic search engines in which thematic searches are frequently carried out by specialist users. The case of Google Scholar is even more perplexing because it withdrew its subject matter classification system in May 2012, removing one of the principal functions of an academic search engine for scientific users.

The way in which an engine gathers the data that it makes available to the user is related to the functioning of the system, and is conditioned by the type of search mechanism it employs. Usually, academic search engines take their data mainly from a crawler that harvests scientific data from web pages and/or from secondary sources that supply processed and normalized data through trustworthy metadata. While there are search engines based entirely on a crawling process, such as CiteSeer[x] or Google Scholar, it is common for engines to use a mixed process in which the web data are complemented with authoritative sources. However, search services such as BASE, WorldWideScience and Q-Sensei Scholar do not implement any crawling process at all; rather, their sources are exclusively recognized products. Focusing only on these authoritative sources, Table 8.6 and Figure 8.4 indicate the distribution of documents

Table 8.5 Thematic distribution of documents by search engine

Categories	Microsoft Academic Search		Scirus		BASE	
	Papers	Papers (%)	Papers	Papers (%)	Papers	Papers (%)
Medicine	12,056,844	23.54	17,166,028	27.74	1,264,705	13.09
Multidisciplinary	9,654,768	18.85			230,322	3.26
Physics	5,012,348	9.79	4,279,880	6.92	497,099	5.15
Chemistry	4,428,171	8.65	5,918,793	9.57	295,907	3.06
Biology	4,135,794	8.07	10,493,156	16.96	1,060,915	10.00
Engineering	3,718,507	7.26	3,980,042	6.43	414,317	4.29
Computer Science	3,555,725	6.94	1,715,193	2.77	671,409	6.95
Social Science	1,928,443	3.77	2,254,685	3.64	1,737,974	18.10
Arts & Humanities	1,373,928	2.68	9,663	0.02	1,566,168	16.31
Geosciences	1,306,235	2.55	780,922	1.26	334,456	3.00
Mathematics	1,207,303	2.36	496,243	0.80	318,730	3.30
Economics & Business	1,019,072	1.99	1,390,416	2.25	743,575	7.70
Material Science	913,818	1.78	5,615,243	9.08		
Environmental Sciences	461,611	0.90	1,337,540	2.16		
Agricultural Science	447,120	0.87	6,438,093	10.40	250,585	2.59

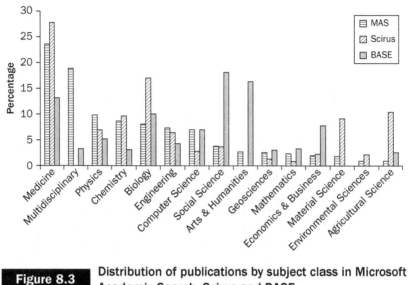

Figure 8.3 Distribution of publications by subject class in Microsoft Academic Search, Scirus and BASE

according to the type of source supplying the data. Five types of sources were defined:

- institutional repositories, i.e., digital deposits from any scholarly organization (e.g., the NASA Astrophysics Data System);
- thematic repositories corresponding to specialized digital libraries (e.g., arXiv.org);
- bibliographic databases, i.e., databases with information on research papers (e.g., CrossRef, PubMed);
- publishing information supplied by the largest publisher platforms (e.g., Springer, Elsevier); and
- internal services, i.e., data from other databases owned by the same organization (e.g., Google Books).

CiteSeer[x] and AMiner were not included because they take their data entirely from the web or from an exclusive source such as DBLP.

Figure 8.4 describes a very different pattern for each service. Scirus is very heavily supported by publisher sources (57 per cent) and bibliographic databases (29.6 per cent), perhaps because this engine is operated by Elsevier. Google Scholar is more balanced, but still supported mainly by publishers (41.7 per cent) and internal products (22.4 per cent) such as

Table 8.6 Distribution of documents by source type

Search engine	Source type	Institutional repository	Thematic repository	Bibliographic database	Publishers	Internal services
Scirus	Documents	7,344,700	4,274,200	25,886,000	49,866,500	
	%	8.41	4.89	29.63	57.07	0
Google Scholar	Documents	8,739,000	12,550,000	5,263,100	30,902,700	16,630,000
	%	11.80	16.94	7.10	41.71	22.45
Q-Sensei Scholar	Documents		2,495,729	35,606,911	6,416,965	
	%		5.61	79.98	14.41	
Microsoft Academic Search	Documents		680,000	40,000,000	14,486,000	
	%		1.23	72.51	26.26	
BASE	Documents	23,224,374	5,056,761	2,963,971	3,381,665	
	%	67.07	14.60	8.56	9.77	
WorldWideScience	Documents	13,078,222	17,997,675	88,361,788	60,569	
	%	10.94	15.06	73.94	0.05	

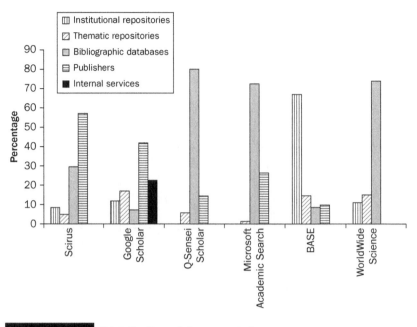

Figure 8.4 Distribution of documents by source type

Google Books or Google Patents that Google reuses to feed its services. Q-Sensei Scholar and Microsoft Academic Search share similar distributions in which bibliographic databases (for Q-Sensei the percentage is 80 percent; for Microsoft Academic Search the figure is 72.5 per cent) and publishers (for Q-Sensei the percentage is 14.4 per cent; for Microsoft Academic Search the figure is 26.2 per cent) are the principal sources. BASE clearly shows its commitment to the open access initiative, being the engine that uses repositories most (with 81.6 per cent), followed by Google Scholar (with 28.7 per cent). Finally, WorldWideScience takes the majority of its data from bibliographic databases (74 per cent) and repositories (26 per cent), while the presence of publisher data is negligible (0.05 per cent).

Figure 8.5 illustrates the distribution of retrieved articles in the principal search engines from 1980 to 2014. Table 8.7 describes two indicators – the percentage of records over the past five years and over half-life – which resume the distributions observed in Figure 8.5. The first indicator calculates the percentage of documents from the past five years (2010–14) in relation to the total amount of records. This can be considered an indicator of relevance that shows the way in which one

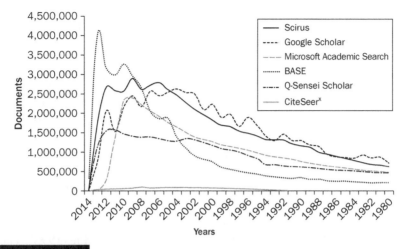

Figure 8.5 Longitudinal distribution of articles by publication date

Table 8.7 Percentage of retrievable articles over the past five years and half-life by search engine

Search engine	Articles over five years (%)	Article half-life
Scirus	11.00	1993
Google Scholar	10.19	1999
Microsoft Academic Search	10.14	2001
BASE	23.43	2001
Q-Sensei Scholar	11.91	1994
CiteSeer[x]	10.30	2001

search returns current documents. The second indicator corresponds to the median in exponential distributions and displays the year that splits the distribution in half. This indicator is related to the previous one and shows the proportion of recent documents in the search engine (Koehler, 1999). Note that WorldWideScience was removed because it returned confusing data with an oscillating trend. AMiner was also dismissed because its interface does not enable the retrieval of documents by date.

Figure 8.5 and Table 8.7 plot the different results for each search engine in terms of retrievable articles by publication date. In general, all the engines show rapid growth in the early years, this being the period of time taken to complete all the records from one year. In this way, the peak point represents the year in which the engine has gathered all the records from that year, making it also an indicator of currency. Then this trend grows following an exponential fit because scientific production increases taking this tendency (Solla Price, 1965). Thus, BASE is the service with the most recent documents indexed, with almost one-quarter (23.4 per cent) of their documents published after 2010. This could be an indication of the currency of the open access materials or, perhaps, it could indicate that in many cases the publication date could truly be the digitization date. On the flip side, only 10.14 per cent of Microsoft Academic Search's indexed papers were published between 2010 and 2014. This underlines the engine's updating problems, with only an annual inclusion of bibliographic data.

Turning to the half-life, Scirus presents the lowest half-life (1993). The principal reason for this could be its closure in January 2014 and the absence of any updating since mid-2013. Another reason could be that Scirus gathered a high proportion of older documents, with more than 14.7 million documents published before 1980. At the other end of the scale, the highest half-lives belong to Microsoft Academic Search, BASE and CiteSeer[x] (2001). It is remarkable that Microsoft Academic Search and BASE have the same half-life when their proportion of recently published papers is so disparate. Looking at Figure 8.5, it is noticeable that BASE displays a strongly unbalanced distribution with most of its documents concentrated in the first few years, while Microsoft Academic Search charts a more constant and consistent trend with a more equitable distribution of items over time.

Google Scholar displays a fluctuating trend with peaks and valleys due, perhaps, to the crawling process and the heterogeneous sources that feed its databases, although the exact reasons for this are unknown. Its figures also indicate certain signs of age, with 10.2 per cent of its articles published in the last five years and a half-life of 15 years. This could indicate that the service is not harvesting as many documents as it was previously, due, perhaps, to better duplication management or to a smaller range of sources. Q-Sensei Scholar displays the second highest proportion of documents from the past five years (12 per cent), while its half-life is located in 1994. Although this charts a less pronounced slope, its long half-life could be due to the inclusion of books from the Library of Congress (25 per cent) – that is, material with a longer life. Finally, CiteSeer[x] presents very similar figures to Microsoft Academic Search, with 10.3 per cent of articles published in the last five years and a half-life of 2001.

Searching

If coverage is the best quantitative indicator with which to assess a search engine, then the search functions are the most suitable elements to test the quality of a search tool and its commitment to user satisfaction. This is because the search interface is the meeting point between the user and the engine, and the way in which these search services demonstrate their technical strength. Table 8.8 presents the principal search features of a search service and summarizes their inclusion (or not) in the search engines analysed. With the exceptions of AMiner and Q-Sensei Scholar, all the engines possess an advanced search form with which it is possible to launch more complex queries that permit high precision or recall. This functionality is critical for any academic search tool because users demand sophisticated queries that solve their specialist needs. Such search engines are forced to offer additional tools such as Boolean operators, tips, shortcuts and filters that facilitate the design of elaborated queries. In this context, the most complete engines are Scirus and BASE because they include all the fundamental elements for the production of sophisticated queries. AMiner and Q-Sensei Scholar have the poorest search instruments, providing only a simple search box for the retrieval of their contents. It is important to point out that two reputable academic engines as Microsoft Academic Search and Google Scholar have problems with Boolean operators – key elements for query syntax. With regard to the number of results by page, WorldWideScience displays the most results, with up to 200 per page, while CiteSeer[x], Google Scholar and Microsoft Academic Search show only 10 results by page, and with no way of changing this setting. This makes the exploration of results time consuming and difficult.

Most of the search engines sort their results by a relevance criterion, which can be simple exact-matching in the case of AMiner or a complex algorithm such as PageRank for Google Scholar or PopRank for Microsoft Academic Search. The second most common criteria are by date and alphabetically by the author's name and title. Engines such as CiteSeer[x], Microsoft Academic Search and AMiner which extract and count citations enable the ordering of results in this way as well. The only exception is Q-Sensei Scholar which disables the ranking of its results by any criterion but relevance.

One other important element in terms of evaluating a search engine is to observe the exporting devices for the results, because for an advanced scientific user it is necessary to export results in order to widen the research and incorporate references into his/her studies. In addition, a huge number of records is demanded by a large number of researchers in

Table 8.8 Search tools by search engine

Search engine	Advanced search	Booleans operators	Tips and shortcuts	Filters	Page results	Sorting
BASE	Yes	Yes	Yes	Yes	Up to 100	Relevance, date, title, authors
Scirus	Yes	Yes	Yes	Yes	Up to 100	Relevance, date
WorldWideScience	Yes	Yes	No	Yes	Up to 200	Relevance, date, title, authors
CiteSeer*	Yes	Yes	Yes	No	10	Relevance, date, citations, recency
Microsoft Academic Search	Yes	No	Yes	Yes	10	Relevance, date, citations
Google Scholar	Yes	No	Yes	Yes	10	Relevance, date
Q-Sensei Scholar	No	No	No	Yes	Up to 100	No
AMiner	No	No	No	No	15	Relevance, date, citations

order to perform bibliometric analyses that describe the evolution of a discipline or institution and test the reliability of the services to that task (Table 8.9). Most of the academic engines export results to the three best-known reference managers in the market: RefWorks, Reference Manager and EndNote. Only Scirus, CiteSeer[x] and Q-Sensei Scholar do not facilitate the use of these tools. With regard to format, the one used most often is BibTeX, with the exception of Scirus which employs plain text and RIS. BASE is the engine that offers the most formats, including MARC, a librarianship format. If the number of exporting records is the most important consideration then only WorldWideScience and CiteSeer[x] make an unlimited number of records possible, while BASE, Microsoft Academic Search, Google Scholar and AMiner only permit the download of records one to one. In terms of page results, these options seem oriented to make the use of the service more difficult.

Access to these materials through librarianship platforms and gateways that connect the records with each user's institutional library is a very important requirement for an academic search engine because ultimately the main aim of the user is to be able to access the full text of each document. Only Scirus, Google Scholar and Microsoft Academic Search incorporate the functionality to mediate between the engine and the bibliographic service that the university library offers to its users.

Table 8.9   Type and format of exported results by search engine

Search engine	Reference managers	Formats	Number of records	Library partners
BASE	RefWorks, Reference Manager, EndNote	BibTeX, MARC, RDF, RTF, JSON, YAML	One to one	No
Scirus		RIS, plain text	Up to 40	Yes
WorldWideScience	RefWorks, EndNote		No limit	No
CiteSeer[x]		BibTeX	No limit	No
Microsoft Academic Search	RefWorks	BibTeX	One to one	Yes
Google Scholar	RefWorks, Reference Manager, EndNote	BibTeX	One to one	Yes
Q-Sensei Scholar				No
AMiner		BibTeX	One to one	No

A heterogeneous sample

This final chapter has described the operation, structure, coverage and composition of each academic search engine analysed in this book in a comparative way. It has highlighted the different searching philosophies of each service and the different theories about meeting users' needs. Discounting WorldWideScience, whose federated model makes it likely that roughly half of its documents are duplicates, and Scirus, which closed recently, Google Scholar could be considered to be the most complete search engine because it combines a deep crawling of the academic web with a wide range of sources and its duplication management is competent. Focusing on open access documents, BASE is the engine which indexes the most papers, which proves its commitment to this movement and evidences its fast growth in gathering its items. Microsoft Academic Search is the engine with the fewest open access documents, although, as has been suggested previously, this could be because it acts as a digital library as well. With regard to source types, most of the engines are based around secondary sources such as bibliographic services which supply the most trustworthy data on bibliographic records; Google Scholar is the engine with the most varied sources, while BASE is supported almost exclusively by open access repositories. Longitudinal data have shown that Microsoft Academic Search is the engine with the lowest rate of updating, while BASE is the engine with the most documents published between 2010 and 2014.

From a qualitative point of view, Microsoft Academic Search has proved to be the best profiling tool, structuring its entire site around profiles at different aggregated levels – developments absent from approximately half of the engines. Based on the search interfaces, BASE and Scirus are the best-performing services, whereas AMiner could be considered to be the worst engine in this respect. Finally, based on the exporting features, BASE is still the best solution across a number of different formats, despite the fact that WorldWideScience and CiteSeer[x] are the tools that allow the user to download the most records.

As has been emphasized throughout this benchmarking exercise, it has not been possible to say which is the best system because that very much depends on each user's needs. In general, the aim of this detailed presentation of each engine has been to observe the performance of each search service according to different quantitative and qualitative indicators, in order to assist with the comparison and contextualization of each service and in highlighting their advantages and disadvantages.

9

Final remarks

Throughout these chapters, a selected range of academic search services has been analysed in detail, working out their functionality and tracking the sources or origins of their data. Thus, with this diverse group of scholarly search solutions this book has attempted to highlight the most interesting tools currently at work in the web environment, emphasizing the particular features of each service when it comes to gathering, storing and retrieving scientific information. From CiteSeer[x] – randomly crawling research documents from the web as a generalist search engine – to Scirus or Q-Sensei Scholar – supplied directly by a specific range of secondary sources, or from the author-centred dimension of AMiner – in which the entire service revolves around personal profiles and their collaborations – to Google Scholar – which, with its powerful bots, sucks up metadata from almost every academic source on the web – this book has attempted to draw a colourful picture in which each particular view on the management and retrieval of online scientific data is represented.

This exploration has confirmed that it is very difficult to provide a general and integrative definition of what an academic search engine is, because although they all contain scientific information and are web accessible, their functionalities and applications differ considerably from one to another. Thus, while some operate as bibliographic databases (BASE, Scirus) others act as specialized search engines (Google Scholar); or whereas some are limited to retrieving bibliographic data (Q-Sensei Scholar, WorldWideScience) others produce elaborated information (Microsoft Academic Search, AMiner). As happened with the dawn of the search engines, it is possible that a unique and clear model of an academic search engine prevails in the future, condensing and simplifying these web tools.

However, this thorough analysis here would not have been possible without the adoption of a quantitative method that has provided a detailed insight into the coverage, sources, parsing and indexing mistakes of these services. The employment of crawlers that have explored and counted the indexed contents – in addition to screen scraping techniques that performed automatic queries to uncover the workings of the search interfaces – are procedures from webometrics that should be extended to the evaluation of information retrieval systems. It is recommended that these techniques replace the usual manual inspection and user testing because they are more objective and include more significant samples. Nonetheless, there has been no response to many of the questions raised in this book, so I hope that these questions become the incentive for further quantitative investigations in this area.

Based on this exploration of the performance of these scholarly engines, a central question arises as to the utility of these services as research evaluation tools. An academic search engine should have no less than a mechanism to extract and count citations in order to be considered an assessment tool. CiteSeer^x, Google Scholar and Microsoft Academic Search are the only engines that could be included on this basis. But despite this, and compared to the classical citation indexes widely accepted within research evaluation – Web of Science and Scopus – these engines still have some way to go before being considered to be trustworthy databases. For example, the limited coverage and parsing problems of CiteSeer^x mean that it does not collect the total impact of the papers and many citations are not properly assigned. In the case of Microsoft Academic Search, the poor duplication control within author profiles, its slow updating speed and the reassignment of papers to other organizations mean that this service is unreliable on personal and organizational assessment tasks. Finally, Google Scholar presents too little control over its sources, making it too easy to manipulate citations.

However, many of these weaknesses are due mainly to technical problems that could be resolved in time, and these academic search engines do offer some original features that could seriously compete with Web of Science and Scopus as evaluation instruments. Thus, the free access, the extension of coverage, the addition of profiling options, the incorporation of visualizations and other benchmarking tools, and the proposal of new bibliometric indexes are significant elements that could enable them to be valued as services with the potential to become reliable alternatives to the classical citation databases currently assuming the dominant position. In summary, it could be concluded that although currently the academic search engines can be only a complement to bibliometric evaluation, they have the potential to become an alternative model for the appreciation of scientific output.

This image of these academic search engines as evolving services which have not yet achieved maturity is reinforced by observing their search interfaces. With the exceptions of the complete interfaces of BASE and Scirus, the rest display a poor search mechanism. Some sites, such as AMiner and Q-Sensei Scholar, do not even offer an advanced search page. It is surprising that as critical an element in a search engine as its search instrument should be inferior, especially considering that a scholarly engine is a specialized tool for expert and uncompromising users who are not only looking for information but who need to build exhaustive bibliographies and locate very specific documents. This problem also extends to the sources that feed the engine because, as with a good meal, the quality of the final product – the search engine – depends more on the ingredients – the sources – than the recipe – the information – itself. Only Google Scholar and AMiner do not provide information on their sources; moreover, they do not allow the user to obtain that information from their databases, seriously undermining any trust in the value of their data. Thus, academic search engines should be explicit about what sources are used in their databases – and in what proportions. This also applies to document formats, because an article published in an international review journal is not the same as a draft paper uploaded to a repository.

In conclusion, academic search engines still have a long way to go, not only as research evaluation tools but as simple specialized search engines. In addition to their technical problems when it comes to computing and extracting citations, authors and organizations – which could eventually be solved – there are other serious problems such as the transparency of their sources and document typology, the currency of their upgrades and the power of their searching solutions which while not as important for a generalist search engine are critical for an academic search engine. I am hopeful that upon the resolution of these initial teething problems in their development these search engines will become a stable presence in today's scientific information environment, building on their strengths and maintaining their position in the future as models for scientific information and research evaluation.

References

AckSeer (2014a) About AckSeer. Available from: *http://ackseer.ist.psu.edu/about* (accessed 22 March 2014).

AckSeer (2014b) Statistics. Available from: *http://ackseer.ist.psu.edu/stats* (accessed 22 March 2014).

Aguillo, I.F. (2012) Is Google Scholar useful for bibliometrics? A webometric analysis, *Scientometrics* 91(2): 343–51.

AMiner (2010) AMiner: search and mining of academic social networks. Available from: *http://arnetminer.org/introduction* (accessed 22 March 2014).

Barabási, A.L. and Albert, R. (1999) Emergence of scaling in random networks, *Science* 286(5439): 509–12.

Bar-Ilan, J. (2008) Which h–index? A comparison of WoS, Scopus and Google Scholar, *Scientometrics* 74(2): 257–71.

Bauer, K. and Bakkalbasi, N. (2005) An examination of citation counts in a new scholarly communication environment, *D-Lib Magazine* 11(9). Available from: *http://www.dlib.org/dlib/september05/bauer/09bauer.html* (accessed 22 March 2014).

Beel, J. and Gipp, B. (2009) Google Scholar's ranking algorithm: an introductory overview. In B. Larsen and J. Leta (eds) *Proceedings of the 12th International Conference on Scientometrics and Informetrics*. Rio de Janeiro, Brazil: Federal University of Rio de Janeiro.

Beel, J. and Gipp, B. (2010) Academic search engine spam and Google Scholar's resilience against it, *Journal of Electronic Publishing* 13(3). Available from: *http://quod.lib.umich.edu/j/jep/3336451.0013.305?view=text;rgn=main* (accessed 22 March 2014).

Bergman, M.K. (2001) The deep web: surfacing hidden value, *The Journal of Electronic Publishing* 7(1). Available from: *http://quod.lib.umich.edu/j/jep/3336451.0007.104?view=text;rgn=main* (accessed 22 March 2014).

Bhat, M.H. (2010) Interoperability of open access repositories in computer science and IT – an evaluation, *Library Hi Tech* 28(1): 107–18.

Bhatia, S., Caragea, C., Chen, H.H., Wu, J., Treeratpituk, P. et al. (2012) Specialized research datasets in the CiteSeer[x] digital library, *D-Lib Magazine* 18(7/8). Available from: *http://www.dlib.org/dlib/july12/bhatia/07bhatia.html* (accessed 22 March 2014).

Bielefeld University Library (2014) BASE – Bielefeld Academic Search Engine: about BASE. Available from: *http://www.base-search.net/about/en/index.php* (accessed 22 March 2014).

Bowen, J.P. and Wilson, R.J. (2012) Visualising virtual communities: from Erdős to the arts. Available from: *http://arxiv.org/ftp/arxiv/papers/1207/1207.3420.pdf* (accessed 22 March 2014).

Brin, S. and Page, L. (1998) The anatomy of a large-scale hypertextual web search engine, *Computer Networks and ISDN Systems* 30: 107–17.

Burt, R. (1992) *Structural Holes: The Social Structure of Competition.* Cambridge, MA: Harvard University Press.

Butler, D. (2011) Computing giants launch free science metrics: new Google and Microsoft services promise to democratize citation data, *Nature* 476: 18.

Chen, C., Lin, X. and Zhu, W. (2006) Trailblazing through a knowledge space of science: forward citation expansion in CiteSeer, *Proceedings of the American Society for Information Science and Technology* 43(1): 1–17.

Chen, H.H., Gou, L., Zhang, X. and Giles, C.L. (2011) CollabSeer: a search engine for collaboration discovery. In G. Newton, M. Wright and L. Cassel (eds) *Proceedings of the 11th ACM/IEEE Joint International Conference on Digital Libraries (JCDL).* Ottawa, Canada/New York, NY: ACM.

CiteSeer[x] (2013a) History: CiteSeer[x]. Available from: *http://csxstatic.ist.psu.edu/about/history* (accessed 22 March 2014).

Citeseer[x] (2013b) Searching CiteSeer[x] effectively: CiteSeer[x]. Available from: *http://csxstatic.ist.psu.edu/help* (accessed 22 March 2014).

Citeseer[x] (2013c) MyCiteeSeer[x]: CiteSeer[x]. Available from: *http://csxstatic.ist.psu.edu/about/mycsx* (accessed 22 March 2014).

Codina, L. (2007) Search engines for scientific and academic information, *Hipertext.net* 5. Available from: *http://www.upf.edu/hipertextnet/en/numero-5/motores-busqueda.html* (accessed 22 March 2014).

Councill, I.G., Giles, C.L. and Kan, M.Y. (2008) ParsCit: an open-source CRF reference string parsing package. In N. Calzolari, K. Choukri,

B. Maegaard, J. Mariani, J. Odjik et al. (eds) *Proceedings of the Sixth International Conference on Language Resources and Evaluation.* Marrakech, Morocco: ELRA.

Deep Web Technologies (2013) How does the number of results work for the different collections, under Collection Status? Available from: *https://getsatisfaction.com/deepweb/topics/how_does_the_number_ of_results_work_for_the_different_collections_under_collection_ status* (accessed 22 March 2014).

Delgado López-Cózar, E. and Cabezas-Clavijo, Á. (2012a) Google Scholar Metrics: an unreliable tool for assessing scientific journals, *El Profesional de la información* 21(4): 419–27.

Delgado López-Cózar, E. and Robinson-García, N. (2012b) Repositories in Google Scholar Metrics or what is this document type doing in a place as such? *Cybermetrics* 16(1): 4. Available from: *http://cybermetrics.cindoc.csic.es/articles/v16i1p4.html* (accessed 22 March 2014).

Delgado López-Cózar, E., Robinson-García, N. and Torres-Salinas, D. (2012) Manipulating Google Scholar Citations and Google Scholar Metrics: simple, easy and tempting, *EC3 Working Papers* 6. Available from: *http://arxiv.org/ftp/arxiv/papers/1212/1212.0638.pdf* (accessed 22 March 2014).

Doldi, L.M. and Bratengeyer, E. (2005) The web as a free source for scientific information: a comparison with fee-based databases, *Online Information Review* 29(4): 400–11.

Dong, A., Chang, Y., Zheng, Z., Mishne, G., Bai, J. et al. (2010) Towards recency ranking in web search. In B.D. Davison, T. Suel, N. Craswell and B. Liu (eds) *Proceedings of the Third ACM International Conference on Web Search and Data Mining.* New York: ACM.

Elsevier (2013) Some people have been asking about our decision to close Scirus. [Facebook status update.] Available from: *https://www. facebook.com/ElsevierConnect/posts/491709367592128* (accessed 22 March 2014).

Fagan, J.C. (2011) Search engines for tomorrow's scholars, *Journal of Web Librarianship* 5(4): 327–33.

Falagas, M.E., Zarkali, A., Karageorgopoulos, D.E., Bardakas, V. and Mavros, M.N. (2013) The impact of article length on the number of future citations: a bibliometric analysis of general medicine journals, *PLOS ONE* 8(2): e49476. Available from: *http://www.plosone.org/ article/info%3Adoi%2F10.1371%2Fjournal.pone.0049476* (accessed 22 March 2014).

Fenner, M. (2011) Google Scholar Citations, researcher profiles, and why we need an open bibliography, *PLOS Blogs*. Available from: *http://blogs.plos.org/mfenner/2011/07/27/google-scholar-citations-researcher-profiles-and-why-we-need-an-open-bibliography/* (accessed 22 March 2014).

Fiala, D. (2011) Mining citation information from CiteSeer data, *Scientometrics* 86(3): 553–62.

Ford, L. and O'Hara, L.H. (2007) It's all academic: Google Scholar, Scirus, and Windows Live Academic Search, *Journal of Library Administration* 46(3/4): 43–52.

Freund, L., Kessler, K., Huggett, M. and Rasmussen, E. (2012) Exposing and exploring academic expertise with Virtu. In T. Gossen, M. Nitsche and A. Nürberger (eds) *The Sixth Symposium on Human-Computer Interaction and Information Retrieval*. Cambridge, MA: ACM. Available from: *http://diigubc.ca/virtu/Virtu_System_Description.pdf*.

Garfield, E., Pudovkin, A.I. and Istomin, V.S. (2003) Why do we need algorithmic historiography? *Journal of the American Society for Information Science and Technology* 54(5): 400–12.

Gazni, A., Sugimoto, C.R. and Didegah, F. (2012) Mapping world scientific collaboration: authors, institutions, and countries, *Journal of the American Society for Information Science and Technology* 63(2): 323–35.

Giles, C.L. (2005) CiteSeer[x]: next generation CiteSeer. Available from: *http://clgiles.ist.psu.edu/CiteSeerX.shtml* (accessed 22 March 2014).

Giles, C.L., Bollacker, K.D. and Lawrence, S. (1998) CiteSeer: an automatic citation indexing system. In I. Witten, R. Akscyn and F.M. Shipman (eds) *Proceedings of the Third ACM Conference on Digital Libraries*. New York: ACM.

Giles, J. (2005) Science in the web age: start your engines, *Nature* 438: 554–5.

Google (2009) Finding the laws that govern us. [Google: Official blog.] Available from: *http://googleblog.blogspot.com.es/2009/11/finding-laws-that-govern-us.html* (accessed 22 March 2014).

Google (2014) About Google patents – Google help. Available from: *https://support.google.com/faqs/answer/2539193?hl=en* (accessed 22 March 2014).

Google Scholar (2014a) Google Scholar help. Available from: *http://www.google.com/intl/en/scholar/inclusion.html* (accessed 22 March 2014).

Google Scholar (2014b) Google Scholar search tips. Available from: *http://www.google.com/intl/en/scholar/help.html* (accessed 22 March 2014).

Google Scholar Blog (2011a) Google Scholar Citations. Available from: *http://googlescholar.blogspot.com/2011/07/google-scholar-citations.html* (accessed 22 March 2014).

Google Scholar Blog (2011b) Google Scholar Citations open to all. Available from: *http://googlescholar.blogspot.com/2011/11/google-scholar-citations-open-to-all.html* (accessed 22 March 2014).

Google Scholar Blog (2012) Google Scholar Metrics for publications. Available from: *http://googlescholar.blogspot.com/2012/04/google-scholar-metrics-for-publications.html* (accessed 22 March 2014).

Gray, J.E., Hamilton, M.C., Hauser, A., Janz, M.M., Peters, J.P. et al. (2012) Scholarish: Google Scholar and its value to the sciences, *Issues in Science and Technology Librarianship* 70. Available from: *http://www.istl.org/12-summer/article1.html* (accessed 22 March 2014).

Hamilton, A.L. (2010) Putting Google Scholar to the test on patent research, *The Colorado Lawyer* 39(5). Available from: *http://www.aallnet.org/chapter/coall/pubs/lrc/lrc0510.pdf* (accessed 22 March 2014).

Hand, A. (2012) Microsoft Academic Search – *http://academic.research.microsoft.com*, *Technical Services Quarterly* 29(3): 251–2.

Harvard University (2014) Harvard at a glance. Available from: *http://www.harvard.edu/harvard-glance* (accessed 22 March 2014).

Harzing, A.W. and Van der Wal, R. (2007) Google Scholar: the democratization of citation analysis, *Ethics in Science and Environmental Politics* 8(1): 61–73.

He, Q., Pei, J., Kifer, D., Mitra, P. and Giles, L. (2010) Context-aware citation recommendation. In M. Rappa, P. Jones, J. Freire and S. Chakrabarti (eds) *19th International World Wide Web Conference*. Raleigh, NC: ACM.

Huang, J., Ertekin, S. and Giles, C.L. (2006) Fast author name disambiguation in CiteSeer, *ISI Technical Report*. Available from: *http://web.mit.edu/seyda/www/Papers/IST-TR_Disambiguation Citeseer.pdf* (accessed 22 March 2014).

Jacsó, P. (2005a) As we may search – comparison of major features of the Web of Science, Scopus, and Google Scholar citation-based and citation-enhanced databases, *Current Science* 89(9): 1537.

Jacsó, P. (2005b) Google Scholar: the pros and the cons, *Online Information Review* 29(2): 208–14.

Jacsó, P. (2008a) *Péter's Digital Reference Shelf: Scirus.* Farmington Hills, MI: Gale. Available from: *https://web.archive.org/web/20081012030944/http://www.gale.cengage.com/reference/peter/200806/scirus.htm* (accessed 22 March 2014).

Jacsó, P. (2008b) Google scholar revisited, *Online Information Review* 32(1): 102–14.

Jacsó, P. (2010a) *Péter's Digital Reference Shelf: Microsoft Academic Search*. Farmington Hills, MI: Gale. Available from: *https://web. archive.org/web/20120314013920/http://www.gale.cengage.com/ reference/peter/201001/mas.html* (accessed 22 March 2014).

Jacsó, P. (2010b) Metadata mega mess in Google Scholar, *Online Information Review* 34(1): 175–91.

Jacsó, P. (2011) The pros and cons of Microsoft Academic Search from a bibliometric perspective, *Online Information Review* 35(6): 983–97.

Jacsó, P. (2012) Google Scholar Metrics for publications: the software and content features of a new open access bibliometric service, *Online Information Review* 36(4): 604–19.

Katz, J.S. and Martin, B. (1997) What is research collaboration, *Research Policy* 26: 1–18.

Khabsa, M., Treeratpituck, P. and Giles, C.L. (2012) AckSeer: a repository and search engine for automatically extracted acknowledgments from digital libraries. In K.B. Boughida and B. Howard (eds) *Proceedings of the 12th ACM/IEEE-CS Joint Conference on Digital Libraries*. New York: ACM.

Koehler, W. (1999) Digital libraries and the World Wide Web sites and page persistence, *Information Research* 4(4). Available from: *http:// informationr.net/ir/4–4/paper60.html* (accessed 22 March 2014).

Kousha, K. and Thelwall, M. (2009) Google book search: citation analysis for social science and the humanities, *Journal of the American Society for Information Science and Technology* 60(8): 1537–49.

Ladd, E. (2000) Chapter 11: HTML forms. HTMLyna. Available from: *http://www.kiv.zcu.cz/~ledvina/vyuka/books/HTMLnya/ch11.htm* (accessed 22 March 2014).

Lewandowski, D. and Mayr, P. (2006) Exploring the academic invisible web, *Library Hi Tech* 24(4): 529–39.

Libra (2007) About Libra. Available from: *http://web.archive.org/ web/20070518163225/http://libra.msra.cn/about.htm* (accessed 22 March 2014).

Lisée, C., Larivière, V. and Archambault, E. (2008) Conference proceedings as a source of scientific information: a bibliometric analysis, *Journal of the American Society for Information Science and Technology* 59(11): 1776–84.

Lösch, M., Waltinger, U., Horstmann, W. and Mehler, A. (2011) Building a DDC-annotated corpus from OAI metadata, *Journal of Digital Information* 12(2).

Mayr, P. and Walter, A.K. (2007) An exploratory study of Google Scholar, *Online Information Review* 31(6): 814–30.

Medeiros, N. (2002) Introducing Scirus: Elsevier's shot at the title, *OCLC Systems & Services* 18(3): 121–4.

Meho L.I. and Yang, K. (2006) A new era in citation and bibliometric analyses: Web of Science, Scopus, and Google Scholar, *arXiv preprint arXiv:0612132*. Available from: *http://arxiv.org/ftp/cs/papers/0612/0612132.pdf* (accessed 22 March 2014).

Microsoft (2011a) FAQ: how are results ranked? Available from: *http://social.microsoft.com/Forums/en-US/5ab1e3b6-9628-4990-9fdd-d21e052e5010/* (accessed 22 March 2014).

Microsoft (2011b) Academic categories in Microsoft Academic Search. Available from: *http://social.microsoft.com/Forums/en-US/bf20d54a-ede2-48a9-8bbb-f6c1c1f30429/* (accessed 22 March 2014).

Microsoft (2012) A new feature for Microsoft Academic Search – the genealogy graph. Available from: *http://social.microsoft.com/Forums/en-US/mas/thread/2be695b7-d9b7-4b55-ac5e-87dc10800858* (accessed 22 March 2014).

Microsoft (2013) Microsoft Academic Search data coverage. Available from: *http://social.microsoft.com/Forums/en-US/mas/thread/7ed5d49d-65b7-4a2f-9adf-4de9e23ee70e* (accessed 22 March 2014).

Microsoft (2014) Microsoft Academic | Windows Azure Marketplace. Available from: *http://datamarket.azure.com/dataset/mrc/microsoft academic* (accessed 22 March 2014).

Microsoft Academic Search (2013) Help center. Available from: *http://academic.research.microsoft.com/About/Help.htm* (accessed 22 March 2014).

Minick, C. (2012) FDsys opinions indexed by Google, *Justia.com: Law, Technology & Legal Marketing Blog*. Available from: *http://onward.justia.com/2012/12/04/fdsys-opinions-indexed-by-google/* (accessed 22 March 2014).

Monaghan, F., Bordea, G., Samp, K. and Buitelaar, P. (2010) Exploring your research: sprinkling some saffron on Semantic Web dog food. In P.F. Patel-Schneider, Y. Pan, P. Hitzler, P. Mika, L. Zhang et al. (eds) *The 10th International Semantic Web Conference*. Shanghai: Springer.

Nie, Z., Zhang, Y., Wen, J.R. and Ma, W.Y. (2005) Object-level ranking: bringing order to web objects. In A. Ellis and T. Hagino (eds) *Proceedings of the 14th International Conference on the World Wide Web*. Chiba, Japan: ACM. Available from: *http://research.microsoft.com/users/znie/f611-nie.pdf*.

Nie, Z., Wu, F., Wen, J.R. and Ma, W.Y. (2006) Extracting objects from the web. In L. Liu, A. Reuter, K.Y. Whang, J. Zhang (eds) *Proceedings of the 22nd International Conference* on *Data Engineering*. Atlanta, GA: IEEE. Available from: *http://research.microsoft.com/users/znie/ icde2006-objectExtraction.pdf*.

Nie, Z., Ma, Y., Shi, S., Wen, J.R. and Ma, W.Y. (2007a) Web object retrieval. In C. Williamson and M. E. Zurko (eds) *Proceedings of the 16th International Conference on the World Wide Web*. Banff, AB: ACM. Available from: *http://research.microsoft.com/users/znie/fp626-nie.pdf*.

Nie, Z., Wen, J.R. and Ma, W.Y. (2007b) Object-level vertical search. In G. Weikum, J. Hellerstein and M. Stonebraker (eds) *Third Biennial Conference on Innovative Data Systems Research*. Asilomar, CA. Available from: *http://research.microsoft.com/en-us/um/people/znie/ CIDR2007-nie.pdf*.

Northwestern University Library (2014) DataBank: article level metrics and citation analysis: Google Scholar. Available from: *http://libguides. northwestern.edu/content.php?pid=295203&sid=2934773* (accessed 22 March 2014).

Noruzi, A. (2005) Google Scholar: the new generation of citation indexes, *Libri 55*(4): 170.

Ortega, J.L. and Aguillo, I.F. (2009) Mapping world-class universities on the web, *Information Processing & Management 45*(2): 272–9.

Ortega, J.L. and Aguillo, I.F. (2012) Science is all in the eye of the beholder: keyword maps in Google Scholar Citations, *Journal of the American Society for Information Science and Technology 63*(12): 2370–7.

Ortega, J.L. and Aguillo, I.F. (2013) Institutional and country collaboration in an online service of scientific profiles: Google Scholar Citations, *Journal of Informetrics 7*(2): 394–403.

Ortega, J.L. and Aguillo, I.F. (2014) Microsoft Academic Search and Google Scholar Citations: comparative analysis of author profiles, *Journal of the Association for Information Science and Technology 65*(6): 1149–56. Doi:10.1002/asi.23036.

Ortega, J.L., Cothey, V. and Aguillo, I.F. (2009) How old is the web? Characterizing the age and the currency of the European scientific web, *Scientometrics 81*(1): 295–309.

Priem, J., Piwowar, H. and Hemminger, B. (2011) Altmetrics in the wild: an exploratory study of impact metrics based on social media. In A. Grove (ed.) *Metrics 2011: Symposium on Informetric and Scientometric Research*. New Orleans, LA.

Quint, B. (2008) Science 2.0 gains another search engine, *Information Today*. Available from: *http://newsbreaks.infotoday.com/NewsBreaks/ Science-Gains-Another-Search-Engine-QSensei-From-Lalisio-50370. asp* (accessed 22 March 2014).

Q-Sensei Scholar (2014) About Q-Sensei. Available from: *http://scholar. qsensei.com/about* (accessed 22 March 2014).

Reeve, L. (2005) Searching CiteSeer metadata using Nutch. [Drexel University.] Available from: *http://citeseerx.ist.psu.edu/viewdoc/downlo ad?doi=10.1.1.68.717&rep=rep1&type=pdf* (accessed 22 March 2014).

SCImago (2014) SCImago Journal & Country Rank. Available from: *http://www.scimagojr.com/countryrank.php* (accessed 22 March 2014).

Scirus (2004) White paper: how Scirus works. Available from: *http:// www.scirus.com/press/pdf/WhitePaper_Scirus.pdf* (accessed 30 July 2013).

Scirus (2013a) About us. Available from: *http://www.scirus.com/srsapp/ aboutus/* (accessed 30 July 2013).

Scirus (2013b) Scirus help. Available from: *http://www.scirus.com/ srsapp/html/help/index.htm* (accessed 30 July 2013).

Scopus (2014a) Scopus | Elsevier. Available from: *http://www.elsevier. com/online-tools/scopus* (accessed 22 March 2014).

Scopus (2014b) Subject area categories. Available from: *http://help. scopus.com/Content/h_subject_categories.htm* (accessed 22 March 2014).

Solla Price, D.J. (1965) *Little Science, Big Science*. New York: Columbia University Press.

Stanford University (2014) Faculty: Stanford University facts. Available from: *http://facts.stanford.edu/academics/faculty* (accessed 22 March 2014).

Stribling, J., Li, J., Councill, I.G., Kaashoek, M.F. and Morris, R. (2006) OverCite: a distributed, cooperative CiteSeer. In U. Manber (ed.) *Proceedings of the 3rd Symposium on Networked Systems Design and Implementation*. San Jose, CA: USENIX.

Tang, J., Wang, B., Yang, Y., Hu, P., Zhao, Y. et al. (2012) PatentMiner: topic-driven patent analysis and mining. In Q. Yang, D. Agarwal and J. Pei (eds) *Proceedings of the 18th ACM SIGKDD International Conference on Knowledge Discovery and Data Mining*. Beijing: ACM.

Tang, J., Zhang, D. and Yao, L. (2007) Social network extraction of academic researchers. In N. Ramakrishnan, O.R. Zaïane, Y. Shi, C.W. Clifton and X. Wu (eds) *Proceedings of the 2007 IEEE International Conference on Data Mining*. Omaha, NE: IEEE.

Tang, J., Zhang, J., Yao, L., Li, J., Zhang, L. et al. (2008) AMiner: extraction and mining of academic social networks. In Y. Li, B. Liu and S. Sarawagi (eds) *Proceedings of the 14th ACM SIGKDD International Conference on Knowledge Discovery and Data Mining.* New York: ACM.

Tarlton Law Library (2014) Google Scholar: case law – legal research process – TarltonGuides at Tarlton Law Library. Available from: *http://tarltonguides.law.utexas.edu/content.php?pid=242166&sid=1999301* (accessed 22 March 2014).

Teregowda, P.B., Urgaonkar, B. and Giles, C.L. (2010) CiteSeer[x]: a cloud perspective. In E. Nahum and D. Xu (eds) *Proceedings of the 2nd USENIX Conference on Hot Topics in Cloud Computing.* Berkeley, CA: USENIX.

Thelwall, M. and Kousha, K. (2008) Online presentations as a source of scientific impact? An analysis of PowerPoint files citing academic journals, *Journal of the American Society for Information Science and Technology* 59: 805–15.

Thomson Reuters (2012) Web of Science: factsheet. Available from: *http://thomsonreuters.com/content/science/pdf/Web_of_Science_factsheet.pdf* (accessed 22 March 2014).

Universidade de Saõ Paulo (2014) USP em Números. Available from: *http://www5.usp.br/usp-em-numeros/* (accessed 22 March 2014).

Valente, T.W. (2010) *Social Networks and Health: Models, Methods, and Applications.* New York: Oxford University Press.

Van Raan, A.F.J. (2004) Sleeping beauties in science, *Scientometrics* 59(3): 461–6.

Waldrop, M.M. (2008) Science 2.0, *Scientific American* 298: 68–73.

Wang, Z., Tang, J. and Gao, B. (2014) How we calculate *academic statistics* for an expert? Available from: *http://AMiner.org/AcademicStatistics* (accessed 22 March 2014).

Warnick, W. (2010) Federated search as a transformational technology enabling knowledge discovery: the role of WorldWideScience.org, *Interlending & Document Supply* 38(2): 82–92.

Wikipedia (2014) Erdős number. Available from: *http://en.wikipedia.org/wiki/Erd%C5%91s_number* (accessed 22 March 2014).

Windows Live Academic (2006) Windows Live Academic home page. Available from: *http://web.archive.org/web/20060412104432/http://academic.live.com/* (accessed 22 March 2014).

Zhang, J., Tang, J., Liu, L. and Li, J. (2008) A mixture model for expert finding. In T. Washio, E. Suzuki, K.M. Ting and A. Inokuchi (eds) *Proceedings of the 12th Pacific-Asia Conference on Advances in Knowledge Discovery and Data Mining.* Osaka, Japan: Springer.

Index